The
Therapist's
Toolbox

The Therapist's Toolbox

26 Tools and an Assortment of Implements for the Busy Therapist

Susan E. Carrell

Sage Publications
International Educational and Professional Publisher
Thousand Oaks ▪ London ▪ New Delhi

For information:

Sage Publications, Inc.
2455 Teller Road
Thousand Oaks, California 91320
E-mail: order@sagepub.com

Sage Publications Ltd.
6 Bonhill Street
London EC2A 4PU
United Kingdom

Sage Publications India Pvt. Ltd.
M-32 Market
Greater Kailash I
New Delhi 110 048 India

Printed in the United States of America

Library of Congress Cataloging-in-Publication Data

Carrell, Susan E.
    The therapist's toolbox: 26 tools and an assortment of implements for the busy therapist / by Susan E. Carrell.
       p. cm.
    ISBN 0-7619-2264-4 (pbk.)
    1. Psychotherapy. 2. Counseling. I. Title.
    BF637.C6 C3465 2001
    616.89'14—dc21   2001000352

04 05 06 07   10 9 8 7 6 5 4

Acquiring Editor:	Nancy S. Hale
Editorial Assistant:	Vonessa Vondera
Production Editor:	Diana E. Axelsen
Editorial Assistant:	Kathryn Journey
Typesetter/Designer:	Rebecca Evans
Cover Designer:	Jane M. Quaney

Contents

Acknowledgments

This book is in thanksgiving to the teachers, colleagues, and clients who have blessed my life with their friendship and wisdom.

I also do not want to leave out Sage Publications, because they hire good people who have been good to me. Thanks, Nancy Hale, for being funny and fair!

And most importantly, thank you, Winston, my true companion in this and everything else.

PART I

Introduction

Introduction
A Resource for Therapists

Your clients, the Hansens, are coming in tomorrow. The first session made you feel like a spectator at Wimbledon; all that was missing was the strawberries and cream. But for all the volleys and lobs, they never really communicated; that was obvious. How can you stop the singles match and show them that it's more fun to be playing doubles, to be on the same team?

When you check your appointment book for the day, your heart sinks. Martin Stevens again. He's so much work! He never says anything; he just sits there looking at you. He makes you uncomfortable. Help me! Do something! is the unspoken challenge, but he won't open up to you. If he makes you uncomfortable, you can bet he makes others uncomfortable as well. He is not even comfortable with himself. What can you do today that might generate a breakthrough in your relationship with Martin Stevens?

Gloria Sanchez is worried. She and her partner are at odds almost all of the time. Although Gloria's assumption is that there is too much distance between them, your analysis is that there's not enough. (One of several clues is that her partner has called her on her cell phone during her past two sessions!) You think enmeshment is the culprit in this relationship. How can you explain this complex dynamic in a way that makes sense to Gloria?

Your Tuesday 1 p.m. client is in the waiting room. This is her sixth session, and her HMO allows 10. The presenting agenda is her impending divorce. Like any good coach, you've reviewed all the plays and patterns with her several times. You have discovered that this woman has old, untreated wounds from her childhood that she will carry into her next marriage and the next after that. You need those four remaining sessions to explore how her relationship with her father gets played out in her adult life. How do you get her to shift her energy and attention from her divorce to her family of origin?

※

This manual is for the new therapist who, graced with a head full of theoretical concepts, now wonders what the heck to do with his or her clients. It is also for the seasoned veteran who needs some new ideas for his or her repertoire.

If you fit into any of the following categories, this book is for you:

- A student in an academic program in the mental health field who sees clients under the supervision of an instructor or professor

- A new graduate of an academic program in the mental health field who has yet to sit in an office with his or her own clients/patients

- A practicing clinician under supervision to meet licensure requirements

- A seasoned therapist who sits in that chair hour after hour, drawing upon all that is within him or her to hear, help, inspire, validate, admonish, and sometimes advise clients/patients

If you are a professional whose practice is described here, this book will enhance your work:

- A solo or group practitioner, surviving outside the managed care system and wondering if the other shoe will drop

- A solo or group practitioner in a managed care system that drains your energy with demands of endless paperwork, including treatment plans and precertification requirements

If you are a practicing professional who fits one of the following descriptions, this book may help:

- Full of energy and enthusiasm, eagerly searching for ideas and information that will make you an even better therapist, all the while thanking God or Fate or the Force for the privilege of being allowed to work with your clients/patients

- Beleaguered, bewildered, overwhelmed by your workload, out of new ideas, and just plain fed up

The Value and Liability of
Seminars, Journals, and Books

I think I'm like most of us who are out there working in the trenches. Since completing my formal education, I have reinforced, updated, and enhanced my knowledge of therapy by attending conferences, seminars, and workshops. I also read a fair amount of pop psychology material, just to keep up with my clients. For the most part, I think that the books one finds in the "self-help" or "relationships" sections of bookstores are wonderful, full of great practical information and ideas for clients and their therapists. Unfortunately, I buy a lot more than I read; it's a time problem. I have a stack of books by my bed that keeps growing; I'm not so sure it's not reproducing. The truth is that I'm good for only about 2.7 pages per night before I cave in to the sleep goddess.

It's too bad about my recreational reading, or lack thereof. As much as I love fiction, novels take a back seat these days. I can't get through what I feel I really need to read just to keep up with my work. And keeping up does not mean that I regularly read academic tomes or those journals full of research that one gets because of membership in whatever professional organization. They are agonizingly slow to digest, and the subject matter is often remote. Back when I had more time, I tried to make myself go through those journals as soon as they arrived. As I got busier, I took to cutting to the "summary" section, hoping for something I could use. I seldom found much. Now, with my schedule, scholarly reading is pretty much out.

I depend on a few seminars every year to keep me informed about current scholarship in the field. And it's amazing how many opportunities there are for such experiences. A lot of brochures find their way to my office, so it becomes a matter of choosing the most appropriate offerings for my practice. I read and save and sort and re-sort and consult colleagues in the process.

Decisions about which seminars and conferences to attend are always hard for me because as a private practitioner, I pay my own way, and the expense is great. The cost of travel, accommodations, meals, and fees for the seminar are bad enough. But usually, it also means one or two weekdays out of the office, so the lost income is also a factor. Attendance at a 1- or 2-day information-packed seminar is work; it doesn't count as vacation! That takes a toll as well because these seminars are usually held over a weekend.

What I look for at seminars, conferences, and workshops, along with the theory and research to support them, are practical ideas that I can take home and use immediately. One good practical idea makes an entire seminar experience worth it. Sometimes, you don't even get one.

The Therapist's Toolbox is a time-saving and cost-effective manual for the practitioner. The table of contents describes each technique briefly so that the therapist can reach for the appropriate tool quickly. Techniques specific to individuals, couples, or families are clearly outlined as well. There are 26 practical techniques and 14 bits of wisdom, most of which the clinician can begin using in sessions right away. When one considers the price of just one seminar, along with the uncertainty of learning something new to do with clients, this book is a bargain. Most of the books in which therapists are interested, self-help or otherwise, explain and promote just one or two new ideas. As far as practicality goes, I hope that owning a copy of The Therapist's Toolbox will be worth several years of seminars and more than a book or two.

Building a Therapist

I had a house built once, and I loved watching it go up. The builder/contractor was a local man named Red. He could have built the house all by himself because over the years, he had acquired all of the necessary skills. Red is not so different from a practicing therapist, and the process of building a house is not so different from the process of building a therapist.

First, the foundation people do their work. Next come the plumbers and framers, then the roofers, then the drywall crew, and, finally, the finish carpenter.

The Foundation

Academicians are the foundation folk for therapists. They are the professors, instructors, and mentors that open their students' minds and pour into them the knowledge upon which the whole project will stand. Theories of psychological development, function, disorder, and treatment are the mix that supports the structure of therapy.

When the foundation for my house was being laid, Red was there every day, not saying much, but watchful, taking in every detail.

The Frame

The framers provide the structure for the project. In the case of a therapist, the framers are those professors and instructors who helped us define the structure of our work. Most of us won't forget those group courses where we dealt with our own psyche as well as peeked into the emotionality of our classmates. In those experiences, we first tasted the fruit of knowing ourselves and knowing others in a different way. In other courses, role playing with classmates and the professor allowed us to put some of the theory we had learned into practice. Learning the nature of the therapeutic relationship really begins in the classroom. Building the structure that defines how a therapist will work with his or her clients requires good coaching, and we were sure glad if we were lucky enough to have an instructor that was a pro.

Red, our contractor, was such a pro. When the framers showed up to begin work on our house, the spring rains came along as well, and virtually all work on the house came to a standstill. The project could not move forward until the structure was framed. When the rain finally moved on, Red motivated, coached, and directed the framers. Working together, Red and the framers got everyone back on schedule.

The Roof

Just as the roof on a house protects its contents, the internship or practicum provides a safe place for the developing therapist to practice the craft. Under the protection of supervisors and clinical instructors, students begin working with the public. Learning to work as a member of a team, making mistakes and recovering from them, and taking some risks are par for the course during an internship.

Dangerous Work

When our house was under construction, one of the roofers, a big guy, lost his balance and rolled off the roof. As he fell, he wrapped himself in tarpaper, finally hitting the ground with a mighty thud. The rest of the crew watched in stunned disbelief as their hefty companion struggled out of his tarpaper cocoon like a fledgling moth. It was a miracle, but he wasn't seriously injured. The next day, the roofer stayed home with a terrific headache. Knowing a delay would be costly, Red took his place, pounding nails into shake shingles like he was born to do it.

On another day, Red was helping a plumber hang pipes in the basement. The plumber, not realizing Red was behind him, swung back his 9-pound hammer, hitting Red squarely on the head. That accident did require a trip to the emergency room and several stitches. Building a house is dangerous work.

Practicing as a therapist is dangerous work, too. If we say the wrong things or make the wrong moves, we can damage those in our care. Every time we interact with a client, our license is at stake, and we are vulnerable to a lawsuit. Physical harm is not beyond the ken in our business; many of us work with emotionally unstable individuals who have the potential for violent acting-out. There is always a risk of harm in our work, for us and for our clients. Accidents happen.

The Finish Carpenter

The work of the finish carpenter defines a house and sets it apart from others with similar structure or design. That is where Red was clearly outstanding.

One day, I discovered a heap of long boards on the floor of one of the bedrooms. A couple of days later, I returned to the same room. The boards were gone, and the room looked nothing like it did before. The unfinished and unrefined boards had been transformed into stunning crown molding. What had been a plain room now appeared regal, a living space anyone would call a master bedroom.

The stereo cabinet he built to hide and house the unsightly equipment of audiophiles became a stately piece of furniture, the focal point of the living room. The front door he fashioned himself was more than we had been able to imagine. Red was an artist.

The clinician who works directly with clients is an artist as well. Where scholars and academicians in the mental health field are scientists, clinicians are artists, creating their own particular style that is the signature of their work. Like artists, no two are alike.

The Therapist's Toolbox is for the practitioner, the finish carpenter of the mental health sciences. The finish carpenter works only after the foundation is poured, the supporting structure is complete, the roof is on, and the walls are up.

Red understood the importance of laying a sound foundation in the construction of a building. He was intimately involved with creating a solid frame, and he could take up the slack when a roofer was injured. He was a coach, instructor, director, motivator, and ethical role model for his crew. But it was his skill and artistry as a finish carpenter that was the defining part of his work.

Like Red, we practicing clinicians are defined by our skill as craftspeople and artists. Our raw material is whoever walks through the door to our office. How we work with that raw material is what makes us the finish carpenters of the mental health profession. It is our ability to connect with our clients that characterizes us. It is the nuances of creating a safe place for them that sets us apart. It is the ability to create an intimate relationship with a difficult personality that makes us who we are. It is the skill with which a couple's conflict is managed, the comfort with which we confront an angry adolescent, and the artistry with which we orchestrate a family session that is our signature.

This book is for the practicing therapist who has the academic foundation necessary to support his or her work. It is for the clinician who has a structure within which such work can be accomplished, be it agency, institution, or private practice, and who works under the roof of a professional organization.

Going Through the Back Door

The tools in this book offer an indirect route into a client's "living space," just as the back door of a house serves as another entrance. Sometimes, asking your client direct questions about his or her life is quite appropriate. But very much of that is off-putting, and pretty soon, it feels like an interrogation.

Entering through the back door is a friendlier, more casual, more comfortable route. Friends call on one another through the back door.

When you don't know what to ask, and/or your client does not know what to say, it is time to open your toolbox and pull out an appropriate tool.

Inside the Toolbox

I have been a practitioner for more than 20 years, and I developed the manual for therapists who, like myself, are working with clients face-to-face on a daily basis. I wish I had found a book like this years ago. With all due respect to theory, sometimes a therapist needs a concrete way in which to use it. I have collected these tools over the years through trial and error. They work for me. Certainly, these ideas represent only a scratch on the surface; there are many more effective techniques used by many effective therapists, but we don't seem to write about them very much.

The tried-and-true techniques in this book are tools for enhancing the therapeutic intervention. Each technique is complete for use in a single session. Information gained from each session in the manual should provide a wealth of material to use in subsequent sessions. Treatment objectives and diagnostic aids are suggested when appropriate to help the clinician meet requirements for treatment planning.

Some tools are as basic as hammers and saws are to carpenters, but their application may be new. Some are borrowed from other craftspeople, and some are antiques that have been reclaimed and refurbished. Some of the tools can be used in any project, whereas others meet specific needs.

To my knowledge, I have not shared any tools that belong to someone else without that person's permission. If one of the tools bears a brand name, I say so and suggest further reading. But all hammers look pretty much alike, and if someone else owned one of mine before it came into my possession, I might not know it.

How to Use the Book

The best way to use the book initially is to treat it like you would if you bought a brand-new toolbox. Open it and examine everything in it. That is, read the whole book. That way, the overall form and function of the tools—their size, shape, and identifying features—are experienced. You may find that you like the feel of some of the tools better than others. You may know exactly what to do with some of them, but find that others are new to you and may take some getting used to. You may want to rear-range the tools by making a check next to those you could use right away, and an X by those you might want to save for later. A few of the tools require specific materials that you might not have on hand (e.g., Sand Tray Therapy), and using others could require approval from your agency or institution (e.g., Field Trips, which are sessions outside the office).

If you are like me, you probably won't address your toolbox so methodically. Instead, you'll want to pull out a tool right before a prob-lematic client walks in the door today, or when you need to change the course of a runaway dynamic in a family session tomorrow, or sometime before facing another agonizing hour with expectant-looking Ms. Nice-and-Compliant. Well, don't panic. It is not necessary to digest the whole book before using it. This guide will expedite your search for the right tool.

Using the Tools

The tools in *The Therapist's Toolbox* are divided into four sections, with corresponding techniques grouped under each section. Each tool (chap-ter) is arranged in the same format: a brief explanation of the tool, instructions for use with clients, materials needed (if any), practice examples (for clarification), and suggested reading (when appropriate). I hope that this format will organize your toolbox so that picking the right tool for the right client will not mean rummaging through the entire book.

⚶

The section called "Hammers, Saws, Screwdrivers, and Pliers: Tools for Every Project" contains techniques that can be used with just about any client one would find in an outpatient setting.

1. *Beyond the Genogram: Sand Tray Therapy for Adults:* This technique works well when it's time to explore your client's family of origin. It allows your client to "show and tell" what it was like to grow up in his or her family. It also works well in family therapy. The children do the work and the parents watch; it's very telling. You will need special equipment for this, but it's well worth the investment.

2. *Who I Am Becoming:* Use this when a client is trying to reinvent him- or herself. It gives him or her a tangible symbol to hold out as a vision of his or her new self. It offers a good way to bolster a wounded self-concept.

3. *Discovering the Inner Child:* All adult clients can benefit from learning to become good to themselves. This model suggests that we all have our child-self within us who can be parented with love, compassion, and discipline by the adult we are now. It is great for people with childhood issues, but not good for adolescents, who are still children themselves.

4. *Dream a Little Dream:* If working with people's dreams interests you but you don't have any formal training in dream work, you will love this tool. It's nice to have even if you are not intrigued by dreams, because your client may be!

5. *The Life Line:* This is a good tool for gleaning a client's life story. It is a quick-and-dirty version of an autobiography.

6. *Family Memories:* Use this tool to get at childhood memories, issues, and traumas. It may provide new information on family dynamics that have not surfaced even if childhood was a relatively safe and happy experience.

7. *Every Now and Zen: Meditation and Mindfulness for the Beginner:* This is "Meditation 101" and proves to be quite helpful for people feeling overwhelmed and stressed by life. (Do you meditate? It's recommended for therapists!)

8. *Journaling 101:* This technique uses the time-honored method of writing as a way to work with feelings. I use this with all clients who are inclined or willing to write.

9. *Favorite Fairy Tales:* This tool works well when your client complains that life has not turned out like it was supposed to. It is especially helpful for people experiencing separation and/or divorce.

The "Grout, Glue, Putty, and Filler: Tools for Couples Work" section houses tools to use with couples. I have found couples work to be a completely different ballgame. Most of my continuing education has been spent digging for effective ways to work with couples. I am so grateful for these tools!

1. *The Couple's Love Story:* Use this early on when a new couple comes in. I usually use it in the first or second session. The couple tells the therapist how they met and why they chose their partner. This tool dredges up any leftover affection between the two.

2. *The Paper Exercise:* This is a diagnostic tool to see how couples communicate and how they make difficult decisions together. It is the tool I use most often.

3. *Between a Rock and a Hard Place: Letting Go:* Use this tool when both partners are entrenched (stuck) in their perspective. It can also be used in individual sessions when your client needs to let go of something.

4. *Resurrecting the Dead Relationship:* This is the best for the couple that has lost that loving feeling. They don't want a divorce, but they don't have much keeping them together.

5. *Jake Got a Dog:* This tool works when it's time to get tough. It's a story that illustrates the cost of self-focused (narcissistic) behavior in a relationship. It's confrontational, so you'll have to be brave.

6. *The Talking Stick:* This technique teaches clear, effective communication. (It's really easy!) You'll need material (the stick).

7. *A Soulful Relationship:* Use this when a couple is beginning to heal. It gives them a way to express tender feelings and dreams of the future. It can also be used in individual sessions when your client will benefit from conceptualizing his or her dreams for the future.

The section called "Measuring Tape, Levels, and Plumbs: Tools for Special Projects" contains tools for specific situations and problems that your clients may have.

1. *Finding a Safe Place:* Use this tool when you are working on a client's fear. You will teach your client to visualize a safe place as a way to decrease fear/anxiety/worry.

2. *Thin Places: A Way to Talk About God:* This tool is great if you are assessing or exploring your client's spirituality. It is nonspecific and non-judgmental. It also works well if your client was wounded by religious abuse (e.g., harmful messages, veiled threats, condemnation or rejection by a religious group or sect).

3. *Enmeshment: Deconstructing the Net:* Use this technique when you need to teach your client about enmeshment.

4. *Rock-Hard Resolve: Holding On:* This is a good tool if you and your client are working on a lack of resolve, passivity, or dependency issues. (A female client says she's weak, has no willpower, and caves in most of the time.) It works well with abused women.

5. *A Matter of Perspective:* Use this when your client is stuck in the way he or she perceives a situation.

6. *Bridging the Gap: Getting Beyond Insight:* Use this tool when your client understands why he or she needs to do something but is stuck. He or she will think through a plan of action and illustrate it.

7. *Field Trips:* If your client was wounded in a particular place or at a particular time, maybe you should go back there with him or her. Also, some clients may be more apt to open up if they are not in the therapist's office.

8. *Rituals and Other Blessings:* Use this when your client would bene-fit from a tangible, though symbolic, declaration of intent (for example, to move on, let go, or declare freedom). This tool is especially helpful for clients with unresolved loss issues.

9. *The Mother Interview:* If your client would like to improve or deepen her relationship with her mother, use this tool.

10. *Necessary Journeys:* This tool gives you a way to help your client reframe a painful experience. Wisdom and strength of character are forged through shipwrecks and adversity, not through smooth sailing and tranquillity. Most people find this tool empowering.

The "Nails, Tacks, and Hooks: Small but Essential" section contains little bits of wisdom that illustrate a dynamic or make a point in terms that most people can understand. Most make their point with a humor-ous perspective; some cut like a knife. Like nails, tacks, and hooks, they carry a lot of weight. It's really best to pick through this whole section and examine each little implement. That way, when a teachable moment occurs, you'll be ready with the right retort.

The Author's Story

The purpose of this book might best be defined by what I am not. I am not an academic. I am not a scholar, and I do not do research. I negotiated the waters of statistics without ever really learning to swim; it was a harrowing experience. I treaded water like mad in psychological testing. But I am a therapist anyway and have remained afloat in private practice without the support of agency, institution, or managed care entity.

I am not the usual registered nurse. I tended to upchuck right along with those in my care and to faint watching surgery. I would sit on my patients' beds and talk about their lives as their IVs ran dry and their urine bags ran over. But I am an RN anyway; my field is psychiatry. I have worked in almost every psychiatric venue and have been a nurse educator.

In college, I never took a course in religion. I did not go to seminary. I am known to cuss and drink alcohol, and I have been married twice. But I am a minister anyway—a college chaplain—and I do my best to serve God, the students, and the church well.

I weave what I have learned from each of my disciplines into my work as a therapist. In the end, the best I can give my clients and readers is my most authentic self. I have tried to do that in this book.

I am forever indebted to the work of those who are all that I am not—the academics, researchers, and scholars who lay the foundation and construct the frame so that the rest of us have a solid structure upon which to do our work.

PART II

Hammers, Saws, Screwdrivers, and Pliers
Tools for Every Project

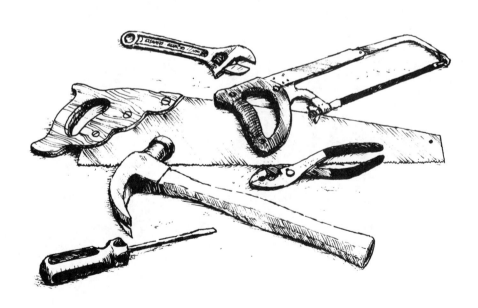

Beyond the Genogram
Sand Tray Therapy for Adults

There is much to be said for using the genogram as an effective therapeutic tool; certainly, much has been said about it. But to tell you the
truth, it has always been hard for me to get excited about actually doing
it. I just never seemed to be able to conjure up much energy for the
"genogram session." Although it is an effective dragnet for collecting
family history, I eventually quit using it.

There is another way. Sand Tray Therapy is a well-known modality to
therapists who work with children. As a nurse clinician working with
adolescents at an inpatient setting, I used it frequently, and with much
success. Now, as a practitioner in the private sector, I use it with all of my
families, and most of my adult clients.

Materials

A Sand Tray

I use a large cat litter box. It is sturdy enough to handle the weight of
the sand, and the walls are high enough so that you don't end up with
sand all over your office. Alternatively, there are all kinds of fancy sand
trays available from vendors who supply play therapy equipment and
other material for use in therapy with children. Some have lids that snap
shut and handles, making the unit quite portable. They usually come

with silicone sand—a finer, cleaner grade of sand. But I find that a litter box filled with about 5 inches of ordinary sand is quite adequate.

Toy Characters

You will need a large assortment of toy characters; I now have more than 200. You don't need a mature collection to begin; a good set of basics will suffice. Consider that acquiring your characters will be a process. I collected mine for several years before I was satisfied with what I had. If you buy them new, they aren't cheap. Garage sales and flea markets usually offer a good assortment at greatly reduced prices.

Because your clients will use the characters to represent their family members, you want to choose characters that will help your clients identify family members and give you a clue about them at the same time. For example, I remember a client who stuck a horse in the sand head first; only the rump and tail were visible above the surface. "There!" she quipped happily. "That's my stepfather!" I got it.

Here's a list of categories of characters that I have found helpful:

- Animals and birds of all kinds—be sure to have a black rubber spider (so often the stepmother); a flexible snake (good symbol for evil; a manipulator, a perpetrator, etc.); some defenseless creatures, such as deer or lambs; and large animals, such as hippos and horses.

- Action superheroes found in cartoons and movies: Ninja warriors, cowboys, Robin Hood, Superman, Superwoman, Batman, Spiderman, knights, Star Trek heroes, military heroes, police officers, and so on.

- Fairy-tale characters, especially princes, princesses, and queens (both evil and good). Also have some mythical characters, such as the Beast (from "Beauty and the Beast"), the frog prince, nymphs, mermaids, fairies, and trolls.

- A few typical people from doll families (found where playhouses and playhouse furnishings are sold). *Note:* Just have one or two of these, because you don't learn much when some ordinary person is used to represent a family member. However, there are those people who don't seem to have anything defining about them, and sometimes, this is helpful information. I call my ordinary people characters the "vanilla lady" and the "vanilla man." Clients understand that right away. If a client chooses the vanilla lady to represent herself, you have a therapeutic direction defined right there. ("Why do you feel that there is nothing special about you?")

- Cartoon characters from current/contemporary cartoons, TV shows, and movies, as well as classic cartoon characters, such as Mickey Mouse and

Daffy Duck. If a client chooses Daffy Duck to represent his brother, I'd probably ask, "What is Daffy Duck like now, as a grown-up?"

■ Fictional characters from current TV shows and movies like *Star Wars.*

■ A religious/spiritual image or two, such as a nun, a priest, a Jesus or Buddha figure, and so on. In one case, a client built a sand mountain, right in the middle of the family, and put a figure of Jesus on top. This defined the direction of the therapy, which, in this case, involved religious abuse.

Instructions for Individual Therapy

I like to introduce this technique with a bit of flourish. Usually, I tell my client that I have an agenda for the session, and then exit the therapy room to get the equipment. I ceremoniously lug the sand tray in first, then bring in the toy characters and dump them on the floor. I keep the characters in a large plastic bin with a lid so they don't get dusty. Because the sand tray looks like what it is (a cat box), it's fun to watch the expressions on people's faces when they first see it.

Invite your client to sit on the floor with you. My clients usually have a look of astonishment on their face, so I like to say something in explanation that will encourage them to engage in the activity. Although each therapist who uses the manual will have his or her own way of delivering the explanation, I suggest something like the following:

I know this looks a little silly, but it is not. This is called Sand Tray Therapy, and it was created for work with children. Children have a lot of emotional content to express, but not a well-developed vocabulary. This gives them another way to express that emotional content. It worked so well with children that some therapists tried using it with all of their clients, and it worked equally well. I use it with my adult clients for two reasons:

1. It encourages you to express an extremely important part of your life in a way that is quite different from writing about it or talking about it. Rather than working from your logical, linear thought processes, you can work from a different, perhaps more creative process of expression. In expressing this material from your past in a different way, you may learn something new about you or your family.

2. It's fun. We all carry somewhere within us that child we once were; sometimes, it's just fun to play again.

So, I'd like to learn more about your family of origin in this session; that would be the family in which you grew up. I'm interested in how it felt to grow up in your family. Your task is to select one of these characters to represent each member of your family, including yourself, of course. Put everyone who was important to you in your family in the scene you create.

That might mean aunts and uncles, cousins, grandparents, and so on. Let your imagination run wild with this; be as creative as you like. Remember, the way things seemed to you as a child in your family is more important than how things really were. Use animals to represent family members if you like. Also, if you have a family member who is or was distinctly two-sided, feel free to place two characters together in the sand to represent that person. All of the characters will stand up in the sand if you just push and wiggle them about like this [demonstrate].

Placement of the characters is important as well. I'm interested in knowing how the people in your family related to each other. For example, if you have two brothers [pick up two characters] and place them like this [stick the characters in the sand close to each other], it tells us something about their relationship. However, if they are like this [now place them back to back and at a distance], we have a very different idea of their relationship. Please try to show me who was or was not close to whom by how and where you position your family members.

Of course, I'm also interested in your explanation—why you chose the characters you did, and what the placement of each character means.

At some point, the client will explain his or her work. Some clients explain their choices one by one as they place characters in the sand. Others wait until the entire scene is arranged before saying a word. I let the client determine how he or she will tell the story. (This is yet another small way to underscore the therapist's role as participant in the therapy process, not the guru with the answers.)

Document the characters chosen and whom they represent in your notes. This session often becomes a foundation for further work, and you'll want a record to refer to.

When the client has completed the explanation of his or her work, and you have asked all the questions you wanted, there is a final, interesting question:

If you were in charge of the universe and could do anything with this family scene you wanted, how would you change it? You can change the characters, their position, your own character, anything. What changes would you make, if any?

This question allows you to get into your client's fantasies about how he or she wishes things were in the family. I always include this part when doing Sand Tray work in a family session.

Therapeutic Suggestions

It is interesting to see how your client will tackle this task. Some get so excited about the adventure that you can't get through the instructions before they are stirring around in the pile of characters searching for their mother. Others will look at you helplessly. That's OK, it's grist for the mill. Find out why your client is stymied. He or she may tell you that he or she never really played much as a child. "Why not?" you'll say, and you're off and running.

There are those occasional clients who truly cannot get out of their (using the vernacular) "left" brains. Venturing into this creative perspective leaves them bewildered. If that happens, I go back to the genogram; they usually have no trouble with that.

If your client is in crisis, use this technique after the presenting problem has been addressed. Events precipitating therapy must be attended first, or your client will not feel validated. In other words, your agenda comes second.

When the intensity of the presenting problem has decreased, and the client is more relaxed, the Sand Tray session may be in order.

At times, it is appropriate to use the Sand Tray session right up front in therapy, perhaps in the second or third session. This is particularly helpful when somebody comes to you wanting "personal growth work," or says, "I would like to improve my relationships" or "I need to learn how to be better at intimacy." These vague presenting problems often result in those moments when you and your client end up just sitting there in silence. (I hate that. Even though I know I shouldn't hate it, that it is a therapeutic opportunity, etc., I hate it anyway. Too many long silences, and clients don't come back; that's my experience!) So, to break out of those agonizing sessions, it's nice to have something up your sleeve. The Sand Tray activity can be a lifesaver. Often, you'll find what you are looking for right there, and the course of subsequent sessions is defined.

Practice Example

Marion sought therapy because, out of the blue, her husband of 12 years told her he did not love her anymore and wanted a divorce. Marion's world was rocked. She deteriorated rapidly and "took to the bed." She wasn't going to work, and basically wasn't eating or sleeping. She refused to take telephone calls or answer her messages. Her friends and family were shocked that this attractive, fairly young woman with a good career would crumble like this. A girlfriend insisted she get therapy and brought her to my office.

After 2 months of therapy and referral to a medical doctor for antidepressants, Marion was much better. She was coming to believe that getting this divorce did not have to mean that her life was over. I thought it was time for the Sand Tray session.

She began by choosing her father first, a cowboy figure on the ready, with guns drawn. "He was always so protective of Mother," she explained. "I'd really like to put Mother in here the way Dad saw her," she went on. "Is that OK?" I told her that was fine. She chose a beautiful princess for her mother. "My dad adored my mother," she said in almost a whisper. "And he still does . . . to this day. Their relationship is one big love story."

Now I had a new understanding of Marion's profound grief. Her father had always adored her mother, yet *her* husband, after only 12 years, did not want her anymore. The model of marriage she had as a child was equivalent to a classic romance, complete with long-term adoration and bliss. But her marriage was over. She thought there was something inherently wrong with her.

A whole new direction for therapy defined itself. We spent the next two sessions talking about her myth of marriage.

Instructions for Family Therapy

I almost always use Sand Tray Therapy early on when working with a family, often in the initial session. In the case of family therapy, only the children do the sand tray work, and the parents are observers. It is very powerful when the parents can see a child's perception of family dynamics. If at all possible, every child in the family who is old enough to grasp the concept should have a turn. In some circumstances, however, there may not be enough time for all of the children to take a turn. If that is the case, start with the youngest child, who, of course, always knows the most! (Obviously, that child must be old enough to understand the task.) Then, pick the one or two siblings who you think should also have a turn.

When a family is in for the first time, I always start by asking each member what brought the family to therapy. I explain to the children that there is no right or wrong answer to the question, it's just that sometimes people have different ideas about what is going on. I try not to begin with the parents, because all too often, the children will just repeat what the parents have stated. Anyway, you get a picture with a wide-angle lens when the children go first; it's much more revealing.

After polling each member, I frame the issues as the family has described them and do some interpretations, if appropriate. Then, I elicit consensus on the presenting problem(s). With that accomplished, it's time to introduce the sand tray.

As with individual clients, I like to present the Sand Tray equipment with a high sense of drama. It's great fun with families because you get to see the kids' eyes light up in amazement as they watch you drag in the sand tray and then dump all the toys on the floor. I introduce the experience by saying something like the following:

Today, we are going to do some very important work. I can't help it if it looks like fun; it's really work [tongue in cheek]. The kids will do the work, one at a time. Everyone has to remain in his or her chair except the one doing the work. I want to start with the one who knows the most, and that would be [name the youngest child—let's say it's Kevin]. Now, Kevin, you come down here on the floor with me. Your job is to make a scene of your family here in the sand. Choose a toy character to be each member of your family. Choose one for your Mom, one for your Dad, and so on. Also, be sure to choose one to be you. You can use animals to be people if you want to. Your job is to show us something about each person by which toy character you chose. For example, if your Dad were big and strong, which animal would you use?

If you are close to your grandparents, or have special aunts or cousins, put them in the sand scene, too. All of the characters will stand up if you wiggle their legs down in the sand far enough [demonstrate]. Show us who is close to whom; if your Mom and your sister are real tight, put them close together, like this [demonstrate]. If they fight a lot, put them far apart, like this [demonstrate]. Then, when you are all finished, I would like for you to tell the story of why you chose the characters you chose for your family. Go!

Therapeutic Suggestions

Sometimes, in family therapy, the Sand Tray session is a diagnostic tool. Sometimes, the process is a healing experience for the family. On occasion, when I take on a new family and we do the sand tray in the first session, so much becomes clear that the family does not need to come back. Surprise! It was single-session therapy! And yes, it takes longer to do this with a family than with an individual. You might want to allow 1½ or even 2 hours. As you use the technique, you will become better able to direct the flow and pace of the session, and to predict the amount of time you want to allot.

Practice Examples

Leona Barton sought counseling for her three children, ages 10, 12, and 16. She and the children's father were divorcing after 3 years of marital conflict and turmoil. In the course of those 3 years, the father had moved in and moved out of the home four times. Finally, he moved out for good and filed for divorce. Leona was concerned that the children were confused and upset, particularly because neither parent was comfortable talking to them about what was going on in their relationship. I suggested that she might want to be in on the first session; she agreed.

At the beginning of the session, the two girls appeared comfortable and curious. However, their 12-year-old brother, Michael, was already in tears. Leona explained that Michael was "the sensitive one" and did not want to be at a therapist's office.

As always, I started the session by polling each family member, starting with the youngest, the 10-year-old girl. I said, "So, what's a nice person like you doing in a place like this?" A little humor never hurts, and it usually helps to break the ice.

Leona and the girls had similar responses; it was about the divorce, they said. Michael would not answer; he hung his head and wept quietly. After acknowledging his distress, I moved on to introduce the Sand Tray work.

With great ceremony, I lugged the sand tray equipment into the office and explained the process. That was the end of Michael's tears. By the time his sister was finished with her turn, Michael was chomping at the bit to have his.

The children expressed similar feelings and perceptions, a sense of loss over Dad's absence, and frustration and sadness about Mom's work schedule. It was clear that they felt she never had time for them anymore. Further exploration revealed that Mom had two jobs, one of them a business venture that required occasional travel out of town. Her response was to complain that on those occasions that she could be available to them, their activities took precedence over spending time with her. The oldest daughter was on the athletic dance team at school, Michael played four sports, and the youngest girl was involved in scouts and two sports.

We discussed the importance of at least some family time on a regular basis. By the end of the session, the family had negotiated a plan. For the next month, they would do something together once a week even if it were just sitting down to a meal together (something they never did).

The session was coming to a close, the toys were back in the box and we were all standing. Suddenly, Michael said, "Can I put someone else in? We forgot someone!" I said, "Sure," and with one sweeping move, he picked a muscular wrestler character from the box of toys and angrily slammed him into the sand. "That's Tom, and we hate him too!" The two girls chimed in agreement like a couple of ringing bells.

Tom turned out to be a business associate of Leona's who had been more and more present in their lives as Dad became less and less present. Now I had new material for therapy.

Leona agreed to work with me in individual therapy. We explored her complicated relationship with Tom, a man with whom she had a love/hate relationship. Although she knew he was not good for her, she felt unable to extricate herself from his powerful influence. That led to her disclosure of the emotionally abusive relationship she had endured with her husband for years.

The Sand Tray session opened the door for Michael to express his anger about an important dynamic in the family that had never been acknowledged, and certainly not discussed. It also helped define the family's need for quality time together. In addition, the Sand Tray session was a segue that enabled Leona to get the therapeutic support she both needed and deserved.

Amy Lin, age 13, was in counseling because she had been acting out at school. In October, she was caught with seven combination locks, stolen from students' lockers, in her backpack. In late November, she assaulted a girl in the restroom and bloodied her nose. Then, right before Christmas break, she forged passes to be excused from class. Her family was shocked and dismayed by this aberrant behavior from a child who had always been compliant and cooperative.

Her mother and father had been divorced for several years, and Amy lived with her mother. Her father had remarried since their divorce, and Amy did not like her stepmother. Her mother thought conflict with the stepmother was behind the change in Amy's behavior. After several sessions with Amy, it was clear that her father's choice of a new wife did not meet with Amy's approval on any level.

I also had one session with her mother and learned that the mother's childhood was more problematic than Amy's. Mom's mother had been married three times. One divorce and subsequent remarriage occurred when Mom was the same age Amy was now. I wondered about a connection between Mom's early adolescence and Amy's behavior. I thought we might learn something with a Sand Tray session.

Amy arranged her family in the sand first as her mother and I watched. Interestingly, Amy wanted to represent her stepmother as her father saw her. She chose a cutesy blond girl character and said, "She's put a spell on my dad."

Then, I asked Amy's mother to do the Sand Tray work with her family of origin. Among the first characters she chose was a witch (from *The Wizard of Oz*). Amy piped up, "I know who that is!" and the two laughed together knowingly. Mom explained, "I hated my stepmother so bad that

I had nightmares about her when I was a kid. I had a recurring dream that she was a witch; Amy knows all about *her*." Then, Mom became quiet and tearful. Amy comforted her by patting her arm affectionately.

The image of the wicked-witch stepmother was a piece of the family culture. At the end of the session, I suggested that maybe Amy could not allow herself to have any positive feelings about her stepmother. If she did, it might feel like she was not honoring, and perhaps even betraying, her mother. By the look on Amy's face, the arrow had hit its mark. Now I had two directions to go in therapy with Amy: (a) the more usual dynamic of the daughter's and stepmother's being "the other woman" to each other, and (b) exploring the family norm of casting stepmothers in a negative light. Mom also decided to do some work with me around un-resolved family-of-origin issues.

Who I Am Becoming

like this technique for the client who has been with me for a while and has made some progress. Perhaps a direction has been defined, a decision made, and/or some discoveries made that answer the question "Who am I, and why do I do what I do?"

This technique emphasizes the process of change already occurring, and it underscores the more positive path upon which the client has embarked. It involves homework for the client and should be introduced at a preceding session. Most of the work is done by the client outside the session; the therapist is an onlooker or kindly coach who supports the client's efforts.

Instructions

Tell your client that you have a mission for him or her, one that should be completed by the next session. He or she is to find some object to symbolize the statement "Who I am becoming." The client will ask you what you mean. This is a good time to recap how things have changed since therapy began. List changed behaviors in your client, remind him or her how a situation was handled differently with success, or how creating a boundary worked so well. Then, say that it has been helpful to many people to have some object, some thing that represents who and how they want to be.

It is very helpful if you have your own symbol to show them. I have a small pewter figurine of a woman that sits on my desk. It is the kind of little trinket one finds in New Age bookstores or gift shops. I explain that I chose my symbol because I liked both the strength and femininity of the woman. She is mythical or medieval looking, wearing a long, flowing robe. She has long, flowing hair as well, and holds a purple crystal in her outstretched hand. She is looking at the gemstone. I tell my clients that she represents the kind of therapist I am becoming—a strong woman of wisdom and mystery.

Tell your client to search carefully for something that captures the intentions of the heart, that is, a symbol that points the way to becoming the best that he or she can be.

The next session will be "show and tell." Your client will bring his or her object and explain why that particular object was chosen. The therapist's task is to emphasize the importance of the client's work. I usually tell my client that the symbol selected can be _life changing_.

Materials

You really don't need anything special for this technique. However, I think it is more powerful if you have your own symbol to share with your clients. It's a good example of the old adage "I wouldn't ask my client (employee, student, etc.) to do anything I wouldn't do," and it shows that you take the idea seriously. It also gives the message that you don't see yourself as a person who is "finished" yet, that you, too, have issues to face and progress to make. If having and sharing your own symbol goes against your grain, don't do it. I know there are excellent therapists out there who do not divulge anything of themselves to their clients and are comfortable with such clear boundaries. I don't work that way. My clients know me. I display pictures of my family in my office (which some practitioners would never do), and I self-disclose fairly liberally (although judiciously, I hope).

Practice Examples

I have seen the most interesting and amazing things chosen by clients to represent who they are becoming, from hatpins to flowerpots. Be prepared to be surprised.

One client brought in a smiling picture of herself taken before she got married. She explained that she had lost who she really was in that marriage, and now that she had escaped and reclaimed her identity, she would never lose herself in a relationship again. The picture would help her remember that.

One summer, a charming, middle-aged woman brought a tomato to our session as a symbol of what she was becoming.

Her youngest child had gone off to college the previous month. She told me she looked up from her cup of coffee at breakfast one morning and suddenly realized that her husband was still there—he was fatter, he was balder, and he was still behind the newspaper. She wasn't too sure she liked him much anymore. She also realized that her identity went off to college along with her child. It was time to reinvent herself, and she needed a therapist to help her do it. It was not an onerous task for this therapist. This woman was what we all look for—bright, articulate, intuitive, motivated, and insightful, and she even followed my suggestions! Before she left therapy, her volunteer job had turned into paid employment, and she was a new person.

Right before we terminated therapy, I asked her to bring in a symbol of what she was becoming. "I was planted as a tiny seed," she explained, looking intently at the tomato. "Then, a sturdy vine began to grow. That vine would be my support system, my family. Then, there I was, all shiny and green. I had a lot to learn; I certainly wasn't fit to eat! Now I'm ripe like this tomato. I can improve a salad or be added flavor to a sauce, but frankly, I'm best on my own, sufficient, enough."

Kate, a college student, said she came to counseling to "build my self-esteem." She was an attractive brunette with large gray eyes and flawless skin; she was also overweight. Kate constantly compared herself to her roommate, who was smarter, thinner, and more popular than she was.

She had relationship problems as well. Mostly, it was the lack of interest from men that was so hard to take. She had been engaged in the past, much to her parents' dismay. They felt her intended was beneath her in a variety of ways. However, the man broke off the engagement. Afterward, Kate realized that her parents had been right, and looking back, she was amazed that she ever considered marriage to such a character. She had another failed romance while she was working with me. Again, the young man was not as invested in the relationship as she was.

Working with Kate was somewhat frustrating because although she knew what she needed to do to lose weight, improve her grades, and get better employment (another issue), she did not seem able to put her plans into action. Then, in session one day, she said that she just did not know who she was, or even who she wanted to be. "I don't feel like I have an identity," she lamented. That was a perfect introduction for the Who I Am Becoming exercise, and I assigned it.

She came to her next session elated. She reported that she had become very intrigued with the assignment and really put effort into identifying, then finding, her object. She talked to her mother and a few close friends about her search, seeking their input. In that process, she had gathered several positive images of herself that she had not considered. For example, one of her friends told her that she should find a cat for her symbol. Her friend thought she was curious about life (like a cat is curious) and that curiosity is a trait that would lead her somewhere, like to investigative reporting, or maybe to travel as a vocation or avocation. Kate loved that idea!

After much thought, Kate decided she liked the image of a butterfly best and set out to find just the right object. She discovered the perfect thing in a small boutique. It was a silk sofa pillow with the emblem of a monarch butterfly on it. She proudly showed me the pillow and said that she was someone who was beginning to value herself, and she was holding out for "true love." She had accepted second best (in the guys she dated) in the past, but those days were over for her. She was like the butterfly, mysterious, mystical, and beautiful. But she was also like the pillow, practical, soft, but not formless. She had decided she was a woman who was becoming strong, but who would not lose her femininity.

The symbol became a focus for our future work together and became an identity that I would refer to again and again as therapy progressed.

The most intriguing experience I've had so far with this technique was with the client who brought in a cow's skull—the kind of skeleton you see in a 1950s cowboy movie that is placed strategically in the foreground of a desolate landscape to depict a bad drought or a relentless desert. My client was a borderline personality disorder (BPD) patient who, among other things, was preoccupied with suicide. We had been working together for 3 or 4 years at this point and had made progress in therapy. I thought the suicide issue was behind us. However, she was not ready or able to let go of suicide as a defining piece of who she was. She had been reluctant to acknowledge that she was, once again, thinking about suicide, sensing that I would be disappointed in her. Bringing the cow's skull as a symbol of who she was becoming gave her a way to express herself that felt less direct than an open admission of suicidal preoccupation. It taught me a lot, mostly about my own impatience with her progress and her ability to pick up on it. Now we could do the best kind of therapy: explore and heal the wounded place in our relationship.

Discovering the Inner Child

There seems to be a wealth of information in the literature about the benefits of inner-child work. Whole books about it can be found in the self-help section of your local bookstore, and chapters dedicated to inner-child concepts can be found in other self-help selections as well. Professional journals document the use of inner-child work, and even trendy fashion magazines have featured articles on the technique. When *Saturday Night Live* skits are devoted to making fun of the inner child, and sarcastic greeting cards poke fun as well, it is clear that the notion is familiar in the culture. However, I have been surprised to find that a number of therapists I know locally, or have met at conventions and seminars, do not use inner-child work in their practices. They know about it, but they have not incorporated it in the clinical setting. Usually, they say they are not sure what to do.

I can't remember just how or when I first learned what I would share with you here. I know it was not in graduate school. I think maybe a couple of colleagues taught me when I worked in inpatient settings. At any rate, I have found this technique to be a valuable tool and have used it for years. I hope you will find it as helpful as I have.

Don't let the length of this tool discourage you. Once you read it, you will see that the procedure is not really complicated. I do the whole guided imagery piece in a single 50-minute session, usually with time to spare. There are suggestions for a following session included in this exercise as well.

Instructions

I do not specifically tell my clients that we will be doing inner-child work. If they know that, then the "discovering" part is not as profound for them. Instead, I talk about doing some guided imagery work.

I live in a conservative midwestern community, so I choose my words carefully when introducing guided imagery. Over time, I have learned that some people are quite fearful of anything that smacks of hypnosis or "mind control." Explain that guided imagery is a relaxation technique that facilitates a connection between dreams, memories, fantasies, and reality. I usually assure my clients that they are in control of their consciousness throughout the process. I assure them that if they are uncomfortable at any time, we will stop. All they need to do is open their eyes and tell me they don't like it.

Explain that they are awake but more relaxed and more in touch with themselves than at other times. Tell your clients that you will be doing the talking during the process; they will listen and conjure pictures in their mind's eye. When the guided imagery is over, you will be interested to learn what pictures came up for them and what kinds of feelings or emotions were evoked.

You probably have a favorite relaxation technique; there are many. The following is the one I use the most; it works for me and may be useful to others. It is not meant to be memorized or used verbatim; you will have your own way of expressing the material.

> Begin by getting as comfortable as you can. It seems that most people relax best with both feet on the floor, and with their hands in their lap. You might want to try that, or you may have a position that is better for you. [Pause]
>
> It is easier to meditate with your eyes closed, so that you can cut out the visual stimuli around you. So, if you are comfortable doing so, close your eyes now.
>
> Notice your body. Get all of your body back into itself. Put your legs into your legs. [Pause.] Put your trunk into itself. [Pause.] Put your arms and hands inside your arms and hands where they belong. [Pause.] And get your head back into your head. [Pause.]
>
> Notice the weight of your body; pay attention to the weight of your feet on the floor. [Pause.] Now pay attention to your legs, and notice how heavy they feel. [Pause.] Notice your pelvis and buttocks and the small of your back. Allow that whole area to just sink into the sofa/couch/chair. [Pause.] Feel the weight of your back against the cushion. [Pause.] Notice the weight of your head on your torso (or as it rests against the cushion). [Pause.]
>
> Now, pay attention to your breathing. Don't try to change or alter the way you are breathing, just pay attention. [Longer pause.]

I go right from relaxation into the inner-child work. The following is the way I move through the experience, and it is offered exactly as I do it for purposes of illustration only. There are many ways to evoke this material; you may want to construct a very different scene for your clients. Feel free to use this, but do not get locked into this one direction. You may come up with something much better!

Timing is important; I have to struggle to talk slow enough so that my client has enough time to mentally develop each scenario.

Meeting the Child

You are walking down a country road. It is late spring. Gently rolling fields lie on either side of the road. The sky is pale blue, and birds chirp in the distance. It was brisk when you started, but it has become progressively warmer; now, your jacket is too much, so you take it off and tie it around your waist. You smell the greening of the earth.

Now you are really warm. You notice that up ahead, the road disappears into a grove of trees; no, maybe it is a forest. Yes, as you get closer, you see that it is a forest. The road takes you there, and as you step into the woodsy arena, there is an immediate change of sight and smell and feel. The forest is darker and dappled with shadows. The air is heavier; it smells moist and rich with growth. The sudden coolness is welcome, like stepping into air conditioning on a hot day. As you continue to walk, it gets darker, not a frightening dark, a delightful comforting dimness, not unlike twilight. Up ahead, in the thickest part of the woods, you see that the road ends. A large iron gate looms at the end of the road. You approach it and see that it opens with a hand latch. You lift the latch and step through the gate. As the gate shuts behind you, you realize that you have stepped into a magical place.

Immediately, you begin to float up into the air. You feel the wind, soft and warm, as you are lifted up. You soar and float and fly. [Long pause here to allow your client to enjoy the flying!] Then, you feel yourself going down, down, down. Finally, your feet, now bare, hit a sandy landing.

You are on a beach. It is a pristine, white sand beach that stretches for miles ahead. The sky is a bright blue without a single cloud. You begin walking. The feel of the warm sand on your feet is marvelous. It crawls up between your toes and warms your skin when you kick it over the tops of your feet. The water beside you is brilliantly blue, sparkling and twinkling in the sunlight. The tide flows gently in and out. The sun on your back is like the presence of a good friend.

Then, you see something move in the distance, way up the beach. It is something small, an animal maybe, or perhaps a child. Strange, you thought you were alone. . . . The small figure takes on a more distinct shape as you get nearer. Yes, it is a child, a child playing in the sand. As you get closer, you see that it is a little girl. [Note: If your client is female, it will be a girl. If male, a little boy.] A little girl is sitting there in the sand playing with some toys. Get a good picture of her. How old is she? What is she wearing? What is she doing there in the sand? As you approach, she looks up. What does she look like? What color is her hair? Her eyes? Your eyes meet hers. See her face. Suddenly, you realize that you know this little one.

She looks at you with curiosity; she is not the least bit afraid. After a moment, she goes on playing. You sit down beside her. Then, you begin speaking. You tell her that you know her well; better, in fact, than anyone else in the whole world knows her. You know her secret fears. You know about all those times when she felt shy and embarrassed. You know about the times when someone hurt her and what that was like. You know about the times when the important people in her life who were supposed to care for her did not. You know when those people disappointed her, neglected her, and even harmed her. You know her happy times, too, all the times when she felt good about herself and proud. You know her hopes and dreams.

You tell her that you have not been good enough to her. You have neglected her and let her down. You are sorry, and you will not disappoint her again. You are an adult now. A grown woman with children of your own [if that applies] who is fully capable of caring for a little girl. From now on, you promise to be there, to care for her and love her and be gentle with her.

If you can, pick the child up and put her in your lap. Hold her and feel her little warm body next to yours. Notice how comfortable and natural it feels to be in physical contact with her.

Now, stand up and lift her into your arms. Start walking back down the beach, carrying the child. She puts her arms around your neck and holds on tight. As you walk, you notice that your feet begin to leave the sand. You are again being lifted up. You are floating up into the sky. As you float, the little girl you carry melts right into you. Your arms are empty now, but you can feel her presence inside you; it feels quite natural and good. So, you float and soar and fly on . . . until you land, once again, in the magic forest. The iron gate is ahead. You approach it and lift the latch. You step through, and the gate closes behind you. You begin retracing your steps out of the forest and down the country road, feeling good and somehow more whole. Continue that walk, and when you are ready, return to this place, here and now. Open your eyes when you are ready, and we will talk about your journey; I am anxious to hear what you saw and what you felt.

Often, clients weep during the guided imagery. If so, ask what the tears mean. You may have to help your client here and offer a little interpretation. I usually tell my clients that I hope they are weeping for themselves; for the little child they once were. Usually, I'm correct. There seems to be tremendous resistance to acknowledging to one's self, and certainly to another person, that the tears are shed in self-pity, probably because self-pity gets no good press. However, people are grateful if you give them permission to cry for themselves; it is an emotion that is pretty common to the human condition.

After processing the experience, you will need to decide whether or not to go on with the next part. I use this next piece if my client has connected with the inner-child concept. You'll get clues if he or she has, which may be tearfulness, animated conversation about the experience, and/or the surfacing of childhood memories. Your client may have several stories to share with you at the conclusion of the guided imagery.

However, if the experience seemed ho-hum, and your client seems only mildly quizzical, or if he or she looks at you in bewilderment (which doesn't happen often, but may on occasion), wind up the session and let it go.

If you believe your client is invested in the idea, continue with this:

> I'd like you to try something for our next session. As a means of cementing your relationship with your inner child, write the child a letter. You be who you are, the adult, and write a letter saying whatever it is you need to say to your child. Wait a day or so after completing your letter, then write a letter back. Be the child this time, responding to the letter from the adult. To help you be that small child, write the letter using your nondominant hand. Bring both of your letters to the next session and share them with me.

Finally, I suggest that my clients find a picture of themselves from their childhood. Sometimes, this means going back to their mother's house and going through some old scrapbooks. I tell them to look for a picture with which they can really identify, one that captures something important. Then, I use my own picture as an example. I keep the picture handy, right in my office. Most clients have seen it but did not know who it was. I explain that in the picture (I'm about age 5), I'm all dressed up so carefully. Ruffles on my pinafore, bow in my hair, little purse over my shoulder. But my socks are a sloppy mess, all scrunched down around my ankles. I explain that it makes me think of how I always try so hard to get it right, but inevitably, I goof up somewhere.

If you would not be comfortable with that much self-disclosure, it is not necessary to do this part, but I think it helps people to know that you have done your homework, too. It primes the pump of their interest in the assignment as well. I ask my clients to bring their picture with them to the next session if possible. Clients usually love to do this. There's something quite bonding about the therapist's interest in childhood photos. Maybe you are the only one who has ever been interested in their childhood.

Instruct your client to honor the picture by putting it in a nice frame and placing it somewhere where it will be seen easily, like on a nightstand by the bed, or on the windowsill above the kitchen sink. This way, she will be reminded of the small child that still lives inside.

A few times, the search for that picture has led my clients to a much greater exploration of memories long forgotten. These clients have lugged in crumbling scrapbooks or shoeboxes stuffed with old photos. I sit with them as they share pictures and memories.

On the subsequent visits, when the client returns with the photo and the letters, simply listen, honoring the work and being aware that you are privileged to be sharing such personal material with your client.

I usually end inner-child work here. There is more to do. For more ideas, check the "Suggested Reading" section.

Therapeutic Suggestions

This is an obvious tool for working with clients who have a history of childhood trauma such as sexual abuse, physical abuse, neglect, and so on. I have found it to be quite helpful for many people. However, discretion must be used. It is a powerful tool, so it can cut both ways (i.e., there is risk of harm). It can go deep into the psyche, and go deep pretty fast. The key is to know your client well. I don't use this until I feel I really know my client and feel that she trusts me. Of course, the trust issue is difficult for the very people who need this tool the most! If your client really believes that you have her best interests at heart, you are good to go.

Of course, the idea with the guided imagery is to empower your client. Any reasonable (not psychotic or severely impaired), well-meaning adult is capable of taking care of a child; therefore, your client is equally capable of taking care of herself. Therefore, this technique does not work well with adolescents or even with teens. They aren't developmentally ready.

One phenomenon that occasionally crops up is that in the guided imagery, your client may feel incapable, unable, or just downright resistant to your suggestions that she is a capable adult. I've had clients tell me that the child did not believe the adult when the adult said she would take care of the child. I've had clients say that they did not want to touch or pick up the child. I've had clients who were angry at the thought that they should have to take care of the child!

Sometimes, this is a diagnostic tool, or it confirms an established diagnosis. Dependent, borderline, and narcissistic personality traits may become quite clear. That's great! Now you have established a paradigm from which to work, and you can help your client understand it.

Once I had a client who despised her child. She was dirty and smelly and covered with sores. The image of the child was metaphorical for her self-hatred. She was the survivor of incest. We used photos from her childhood, art therapy, dolls, and a trip to a playground to help her change her concept of the dirty little girl.

Materials

If you are new to relaxation and guided imagery, you might want to read the illustrations right from the book at first. I did that. Actually, I wrote the material myself and then read it. Call it stage fright. It worked fine. Clients don't know that not everyone does it that way; anyway, their eyes are closed!

I find soothing music to be helpful for this work. The music creates a serene, mellow atmosphere, and it helps with distracting noises, such as ringing phones, traffic, noise in the waiting room, and so on. Although I have soft music going in my office all the time, I use a portable CD player right in the therapy room for relaxation and guided imagery. The music sounds much more present and helps set the stage for something special.

Practice Examples

Grace was an attractive woman in her early 40s who sought therapy for "relationship problems." At a glance, it looked like she had it all. She was tall and thin, her blond hair cut in a stylish crop. She dressed beautifully and was a successful interior designer with her own business. She drove new cars and lived in a prestigious neighborhood. She was a single mother of two teenagers and was seldom without a man in her life. However, she was miserable.

She had been married twice, and since her second divorce, she had had serious liaisons with several men, but none worked out. The last breakup was recent, and the pain of losing the relationship (although Grace was the one who broke it off) was the catalyst that motivated her to seek counseling.

Her success in interior design was hard-won. She had always had a knack for color and design but did not have a college degree. Instead, she apprenticed with a local designer, who recognized something special in the determined young woman and decided to give her a chance. Grace worked 6 years for her mentor, and when the elder woman retired, she helped Grace buy the business by carrying the loan. Buying the business was a huge risk. She was on her own at the time, recently divorced from her first husband, but owning the business could give her the financial security and social legitimacy for which she longed.

Grace was from the wrong side of town. She grew up in a poor, chaotic family with a mother who "could never feel her children." Partly, that was because she was so immersed in first one, then another, alcoholic or abusive relationship. Her children were outside the circle of her attention, which was riveted to whatever man occupied the eye of the hurricane. As a young girl, Grace vowed to live a different life from the one in which she grew up. She was embarrassed by her neighborhood, her secondhand clothes, her weirdly intense mother, and her mother's many men.

On one hand, as an adult, she did escape the poverty and low social position of her childhood, but on the other, she was repeating her mother's life.

It took a long time to get beyond dealing with the crisis du jour in our sessions. Within 2 years, she had three significant relationships. She brought them all to her therapy sessions sooner or later, and the silhouette of a pattern began to take shape. At first, she idealized her new boyfriend. He was "the one" at last! He was smart, successful, fun, admirable, and so on. She was particularly besotted if the man did not seem all that interested in her; it was as if the bell sounded, the gates opened, and the race was on. Once won, the prize lost its luster.

The man always fell madly in love with her and soon began talking about ceremonies, rings, and a shared life. About that time, Grace would fall apart. She'd become angry with her lover for not taking good enough care of her, and she'd start going out with her single girlfriends again. She would nurture new attractions and flirt with strangers. Basically, she would sniff around for new material. Then, she would weep in sessions and berate herself for not being able to make a relationship work. She would bring the poor guy in for a couples session, and he would predictably declare his heart and agree to do whatever it took to make things work. She was always able to convince the man, herself, and me that if he would just be more understanding of her needs, she could go forward with the relationship. A period of individual sessions with the guy along with couples work would ensue. During these times, Grace and I could do some work on intimacy, including family-of-origin work and attachment issues. At one such time, I introduced her to inner-child work as described here.

During the exercise, she chose to lie on the couch. In the guided imagery, upon discovery of the child, she wept silently. The tears ran out the corners of her eyes, and every now and then, she wiped them away. At the end of the exercise, I asked her if she could talk about the tears. She explained that the experience elicited profound sadness on several levels. First was pity for the little girl who had had so little real mothering. When the little girl sitting in the sand first saw the adult woman walking toward her, she immediately wondered what she should do to please/ entertain/engage the woman; certainly, she couldn't play anymore. The role reversal that defined her relationship with her mother began much earlier than Grace had realized. Second, the image of her adult self and her child self was superimposed with the image of her and her mother. Just as the child and the adult were really images of the same person, maybe she and her mother were the same person as well. Her greatest fear was that she would somehow turn out to be just like her mother, and although she saw herself as a better mother to her children than her mother had been to her, her pattern with men was exactly like her mother's. Third was the awareness that the child doubted that the adult could or would really take care of the child. This insight allowed me to begin some hard work on Grace's reluctance to assume responsibility for her own behavior.

Grace remained in therapy, off and on, for a long time, but the inner-child work was a powerful tool. Prior to the exercise, Grace wanted to focus her energy and her therapy time on the most recent issue with the most recent lover. Now, I no longer had to push for addressing childhood issues. She understood all too well that her issues with men weren't just about the lousy men who were available these days, but were also about the way she related to herself and to others.

Dream a Little Dream

Most people are interested in their dreams. I am very interested in dreams myself. I even have a bit of a reputation for interpreting dreams around the campus where I work as a chaplain. Students e-mail me or come knocking on my door, eager to share their nocturnal musings. My skills were not developed in the classroom or laboratory; they fall into the "knack" or "gift" category. Frankly, quite by accident, I am good at it.

Unfortunately, I do not remember my own dreams very often. It is frustrating because people are forever sharing their rich and varied dreams and dream sequences with me, and I get so few of my own; always the bridesmaid, never the bride.

To improve my dream expertise, I read a few books and attended a seminar. I did learn some nice tricks and techniques, although I am convinced that dream work is more an art than a science.

I use what I know about dreams regularly with those clients who are interested in or inclined toward working with their dream lives. I hope the following will get you started or enhance what you are already doing.

Instructions

More often than not, clients initiate dream work. "I had the strangest dream last night," they'll say, or "I have this recurrent dream . . . ," or "Do you think dreams are important?" On occasion, I introduce the idea of working with dreams. I may ask about the client's dream life, or suggest that we explore dreams if we are stuck.

Of course, you have to have a dream or two with which to work in the first place. If your client is interested in working with dreams, but does not have any offerings to explore, you can try generating some dreams.

Dream Incubation

Help your client hatch a dream or two by using this technique as a guide. Remember that each therapist using the manual will have his or her own way of delivering the instructions.

> Before going to bed, spend a little time thinking about what you would like to dream. If you are seeking the answer to a particular question or guidance in making a decision, or you want to explore something personal, consider the issue thoughtfully. If you are a person who prays, this would be the time to pray. Ask for guidance, direction, or insight from your dream. Also ask that you will be able to record or remember your dream.
>
> Next, write a brief description of your quest or area of concern on a piece of paper. Describe what it is you want, and place the paper under your pillow.

I was a card-carrying skeptic when I first heard about dream incubation, but when I tried it myself, it worked! If you have similar misgivings, give it a test run. I find that I can't teach my clients anything that I can't believe in myself, so if this does not work for you, you might not want to recommend it.

Record the Dream in Writing

Place a notepad or tablet and pen near your bed. Some people like to keep their pen and paper on the bedside table; others find having their notepad and pen right beside them on the bed the best method. The point is to wake up enough to record your dream as soon after you have it as possible. There are those who have no problem getting up, turning on the light, donning glasses, and recording their dream. Others find that sacrifice much too great and are doing well to grasp the pen and scribble a brief description of their dream without ever raising head from pillow. Actually, the latter method usually works well enough. The next morning, the few scribbled words may be enough to cue the dreamer into remembering the storyline. The tale can be expanded and recorded in the light of day.

Interpretation

The best interpreter for a dream is the dreamer. Always ask your clients what they think their dreams mean. That does not mean that you shouldn't offer your take on the dream. Just let your clients know that their interpretation is probably the most accurate or important, but you would like them to consider yours as well.

If you get interested in dream interpretation, you might want to do some studying. There are books to read and seminars to attend. Some books offer help by describing and analyzing dream symbols. Dream analysts propose the metaphorical meanings of dream themes and objects. But if you just can't pursue the additional knowledge right now, don't be afraid to do what you can with dreams. It is rich soil for the most meager seed.

Dream Journaling

I tell my clients about dream journaling so that they have the option if dream work interests them. As the name implies, the dreamer keeps a record of his or her dreams over time.

When I did this myself, it was a fascinating experience. Themes began to emerge, and I got in touch with issues that my unconscious mind was trying to work out. As you might guess, the issues were those that I could not successfully work out in my conscious mind.

I suggest that clients get a spiral notebook, or one of those lovely blank hardcover books, to do their journaling. After several dreams are documented, I have them go back through their work and highlight similar themes, or objects or situations, that symbolically suggest themes. Then, I invite them to bring their journals to session, and we review the work.

Dream Groups

When I took a seminar on dream work several years ago, many of the participants were members of a dream group. These six or eight women had been meeting together for a couple of years once a month to share their dream journals and work with on one another's dream material. None of them was a psychology professional; they were just bright, articulate, interested women. They told me that the group had become a wonderful source of strength and support for all of them. I love the idea of a dream group and tell my clients about it, hoping that the idea will eventually spark in one of them and ignite the creation of a group.

Practice Examples

Suzanne was a 39-year-old internist who worked in a large hospital. The group of hospital internists hired her immediately upon the completion of her residency at a teaching institution. She had been working with the group for 4 years when the hospital moved to the managed care model and purchased all of the physician groups. Now she was an employee of the hospital. The transition from the physician-owned and -operated group practice to the new model was agonizing for everyone.

She entered therapy because, as a single woman with no family in the area, she had no safe place to work through her frustrations. Most of her friends had connections to the hospital and her work. She had enjoyed close relationships with the 11 other doctors in her group and knew their wives, husbands, and children. For a variety of reasons, she was not comfortable sharing information about the realities of her situation at the hospital and clinic with people outside the system. Chief among them was that she did not want to be perceived as a whiner and complainer. Also, she feared becoming known as a malcontent. The very large hospital in the relatively small community had eyes and ears everywhere. Job security was an issue.

In therapy, she lamented that the doctors had less and less control over the care of their patients. The hospital, which owned the major managed care program in the area, dictated their every move, and profit was always the bottom line. As the doctors in her group slowly lost control over how they practiced medicine and managed their incomes, tension rose. Eventually, Suzanne and one of her colleagues became locked in conflict.

Allen, a 56-year-old partner in the group, was difficult in the first place. He was a controlling type who longed to be in charge of the group. His sense of entitlement was noxious to others, so his peers never chose him as the chairman. But he was a brilliant physician whose knowledge and skill were assets to the group. He had his good moments, but his intense need to run the show made others uncomfortable around him.

As more and more control was wrested from the doctors, Allen's need for control soared. He plotted and planned and came up with one scheme after another, which he presented at the group's meetings. Sometimes, his ideas had merit, but more often than not, he could not achieve consensus among the others. Finally, he targeted Suzanne, certain he could make her an ally.

At first, Suzanne was unsuspecting and flattered when one of the old guard took an interest in nurturing a relationship with her. They had lunch together and conferred about their problem patients. They visited one another's offices on occasion and traded being on call now and then. They discussed hospital politics. Over time, Suzanne learned more about the practice of medicine and the operation of their group. More and more, her opinion and perspective on practice issues and group and hospital politics differed from Allen's. As her confidence grew and she found her voice, he liked her less and less. Finally, she embarrassed him in a group meeting by disagreeing with him. The other members agreed with her, and his proposal was summarily dropped. It marked the beginning of the end of their comfortable relationship. Now, he was determined to have the upper hand with her, and she was equally determined not to let him have it.

Throughout the next year, Allen was the subject of many conversations in my work with Suzanne. Conflict with an intimate was new to her. Her parents were loving and respectful to each other, and she had close relationships with her brother and sister. She had a professor in medical school that treated her with disdain because she was female, but she did not take that personally; he treated all of the female medical students that way. She had her share of lovers and breakups, but when things got bad enough, she was able to cut her losses and move on. She had never had serious conflict with a peer or others in her work setting. The ongoing angst with Allen was new to her.

We worked on her relationship with her father and brother. We did inner-child work. As a religious person, she prayed, worked on forgiveness, and learned to meditate. We did self-esteem work as well. Her damaged relationship with one of her partners was not the prevailing theme in her therapy, but it was always buzzing around, like an annoying bug.

Then, one day, we explored her dream life and talked about dream incubation, recording dreams, and dream journaling. She brought this dream to a subsequent session:

> I was at a street fair. I was alone, but it didn't seem to bother me. I walked around looking at stuff—art booths and soda vendors and cotton candy machines. There were children with balloons and old ladies in wheelchairs. I noticed a large area ahead; tables and chairs all set up; it was an area for eating, like picnic grounds. . . . I saw Allen sitting there with a little boy. Strange, I thought, Allen has two daughters. But anyway, it was a boy, his son. So, I went over to him and sat down next to him. He looked so sad! He was overdressed for a picnic; his suit jacket was on the back of the chair. He had on a heavily starched white shirt and a tie. But his face was so sad! I asked him what was wrong. He said his wife was leaving him. He didn't want her to, but she was anyway. He leaned his head on my shoulder. I put my arm around him. (I thought, good night! I'm putting my arm around Allen! This is strange! But even thinking that, I did it anyway. It wasn't so bad. . . .) Then, I noticed the little boy again. He just sat there; didn't go play with the other kids or anything . . . just sat there looking like a geeky kid, watching the other kids play.

Suzanne had a pretty good read on her dream. She felt that it was about her desire to have a more positive relationship with Allen. The festival scene represented her desire for that, the celebratory nature of a better relationship. The way he was overdressed was about his inappropriate behavior in many venues. The part about his wife leaving him was about his knowledge of not being well liked and his fear of being left. She also thought maybe it was about her own abandonment fears that we had been talking about in therapy.

She could not figure out why the little boy was there. I wondered if it could be Allen's own little boy self, the remnant of a painful past, a little boy who was left out and not admired by his peers. Could that be about Suzanne as well? A sense of not belonging had been a pervasive theme in her life.

I thought the comforting gesture of putting her arm around the boy might be her desire to be her best self with Allen. Perhaps, on some level, she wished she could care for and comfort this noxious person in her life. Perhaps she longed for that same caring response for the noxious parts of herself. Maybe she and Allen were not so different after all.

The dream was an epiphany experience that allowed her to release a lot of the angst that characterized her every response to Allen.

James started seeing me for therapy during his junior year in college. He had been feeling depressed all semester and was plagued with generalized anxiety. One night, he awoke with classic symptoms of panic. When it happened again in a history class and he had to leave the lecture hall, he sought therapy.

He was bright and funny, although quite narcissistic. His mother, a widow, doted on her youngest child and only son. His father died when James was 9 years old, and his hard-working mother supported and raised James and his two sisters alone.

He had one or two good friends in college, but he was introverted and ill at ease around groups. He was somewhat interested in girls but did not seem willing or able to do what was necessary to get a date. He asked a girl in his geography class to have coffee with him, but his interest fizzled when he found out that she smoked cigarettes.

We worked on his father's death and his relationship with his mother and sisters. We talked about abandonment and self-esteem. We talked about intimacy. Then, one day, he came to session with a burning agenda. Would I help him understand a dream he had a few nights ago?

I was in one of the classroom buildings on campus and I needed to go to the bathroom. I saw the restroom sign and symbols for the men's and women's bathrooms. I went into the women's. I knew it was not where I was supposed to be, but I felt quite comfortable there. I was curious, too. I looked in each stall, just kind of nosing around to see what was what. Then, my sister came in. She was shocked and horrified that I was there. She grabbed me by the arm and started pulling me toward the door. I didn't want to leave. I resisted her tugging at me.

I thought I knew immediately what the dream symbolized and was amazed that James was so blind to it. Clearly, he was identifying with the domain of women. He was comfortable, curious, and drawn to exploring female territory. If he identified with the female side of himself, wouldn't he be attracted to men?

His sister's resistance to his position or place in the women's restroom could be about the certain reaction of his mother if his sexual identity was homosexual. Her staunch fundamentalist Christian perspective was well known to her son. Homosexuality was forbidden, a sin. His sister's tugging at him could represent his own resistance to coming out, even to himself.

I wasn't about to interpret this for him. If he could not discern the suggestion of homosexuality implied by the dream, then he wasn't ready for the discovery. Also, I might have been wrong. I questioned him and probed around to see if he could or would come to his own interpretation, but he was completely stumped. We let it go.

The dream informed my work with James, even though I did not say anything about my suspicions to him. I was intentional about letting him know my position on gays, lesbians, bisexuals, and transgendered people so that if he were gay, he would know that I was safe and supportive. About 10 months later, he came out to me and to himself. He stayed in therapy through the stormy times that followed. There was his first gay relationship and coming out to his mother and sisters. There was graduation from college and securing his first job. Although there was pain and struggle in these transitions, shortly after he acknowledged his true identity, the panic attacks disappeared, along with the nagging anxiety, and his depression improved.

The Life Line

Most therapist types have to write a detailed autobiography at some point during training; I did. It was an assignment that I actually still remember, although no telling what happened to the final product. All that is said about the importance of writing proved to be true. When the memories and fleeting pictures of my past were organized, recounted, and documented on paper, I felt a greater sense of ownership in my own life experience.

In the process of writing, memories that once seemed isolated or unrelated fell into place as essential pieces of the whole. Particular events took on new meaning when viewed in retrospect. The relative importance of things seemed to shift. The big occasions became smaller and less meaningful, whereas the small moments loomed large and formative. When I was finished, I knew myself better.

If we can facilitate this experience for our clients, we allow them to participate in the same self-awareness. Self-awareness leads to wholeness. Wholeness leads to acceptance. Acceptance leads to empowerment. Self-awareness, wholeness, and acceptance enhance the possibility of intimacy with self. Intimacy with self enhances intimacy with other.

At the beginning of my work as a private practitioner, I assigned the autobiography, but I ran into trouble. Either I had a client who abhorred the writing process and I did not know it, or I had a perfectionist-compulsive-please-the-teacher type. If the client hated to write, the assignment would go undone. There would be a couple of sessions of the "oh-I-forgots," followed by one or two of the "gee-I'm-sorrys," followed by "I-won't-mention-it-and-maybe-she'll-forget." On the other hand, if a client took the assignment to heart, I received autobiographical tomes. I'll never forget the proud face of the lady who carted in a 98-page epistle. Reading homework outside the therapy office is not cost-effective! The autobiography assignment was short-lived in my repertoire.

The Life Line technique that follows does a good job of encapsulating the benefits of the autobiography in a way that is both acceptable and valuable to most clients, and it requires no out-of-session work for the therapist.

Instructions

Tell your clients that you are interested in all of the important events in their lives. Explain that early events can be formative and may very well be coloring perceptions or situations in life right now. At any rate, the quest for self-knowledge involves an integration of the past and the present, so an exploration of a person's history is an important therapeutic direction.

I like to provide my clients with large sheets of drawing paper for this technique, so I pull out a few at this point. Instruct your clients to draw a diagonal line across the page from one corner to the opposite corner. Then, using hash marks, they should mark the significant events in their lives. I think it is also helpful to document the time, either by year or by how old they were at the time of the event. The event or situation should be named as well. For example, "1968—sister Robin born," or "age 7— sister Robin born."

They should begin with their earliest memory and end with the present. Emphasize that you are interested in what they perceive as the *significant* events; therefore, both positive and negative experiences should be considered. I encourage my clients not to be limited by strict adherence to exact chronological order. In other words, they shouldn't worry about which year in high school they ran for office and lost, but, rather, document "high school—ran for Social Director and lost."

I don't give them too much more information than that; that way, clients are free to either stay with a brief overview of their lives or really go in depth. It is interesting and informative to see just what they do with the assignment. Sometimes, one large sheet of drawing paper is enough, but not always; I send my clients home with several. Actually, regular 8½ × 11 paper will work if that's all you have around, but I think the large paper helps to underscore the importance of the work.

Your clients bring their work back to session when they are finished. I usually ask when they think the assignment will be completed. Most people want a couple of weeks.

Processing the Life Line usually takes at least one session. I ask my clients to spread the paper out on the floor so that we can both see it, and then we go through each event that they have documented.

Practice Examples

Mary had been in therapy with me for more than a year. Usually, I do the Life Line much earlier, but not with Mary. Trust was such a huge issue with her, and her childhood had been so traumatic, that I was afraid the Life Line technique could push her into disclosing events before she was ready.

As a child, Mary had been sexually abused by a sadistic older stepbrother and, later, by his friends as well. By the time he brought in his friends, little Mary was so terrorized that any hope of her reaching out for help was long gone. She endured semiritualized abuse from these boys for several years. Finally, as a teenager, Mary told her mother the truth. Her mother did not believe her.

Mary was a lesbian in a stable relationship of some years with a compassionate and supportive partner, but their life together had to be kept secret in the conservative rural community where they lived. The potential for criticism and outright rejection should Mary's sexual preference become known re-created the same fears with which she lived as a child. Now, she was having frequent nightmares, and she had experienced several episodes of losing time.

After months of therapy, I felt our relationship was well established, so I decided to try the Life Line. It took several sessions to process her work. As one would guess, she had many stories to tell. Although she could not write down a history of her abuse on paper, the Life Line became a structure that supported disclosure of deeply held secrets. The events she documented served as springboards that led to a verbal recounting of the abuse to me.

Through the course of processing the Life Line, I learned that when she was growing up, Mary spent many summers with her Aunt Pat, who lived in St. Louis, miles away from Mary's home. Those summers with her Aunt Pat were spent going to museums, movies, restaurants, and the zoo. Aunt Pat's attention and affection probably saved Mary's emotional life. Learning about those summers was like finding a gold nugget in a miner's pan; I had something to take to the bank. I used the memories of those summers as a way for Mary to establish a safe place inside herself (see Chapter 18, "Finding a Safe Place"). Through guided imagery, Mary learned to go back and reclaim a positive childhood memory. Her ability to resurrect that memory and sense of well-being was useful in combating her almost constant sense of fear. Although it did not save Mary from more years of therapy and more than one hospitalization, it served a valuable purpose in our relationship and in helping her manage her symptoms.

Bob, a 58-year-old high school principal, came to therapy because of a conflict with his sister. In the first session, he assured me that it would be the last. He was accustomed to solving his own problems, thank you very much, but this time, he was stuck. He would get the advice of a professional and be on his way. In that first session, I learned about the nature of the conflict: His sister had accused him of being "insensitive." I also learned a little about his life. As it turned out, this was not the first time he had been tagged as insensitive. When I suggested that perhaps a pattern was evident, he was intrigued and signed on for "another session or two."

I learned very quickly that Bob liked to do things his way. He was not very interested in the direction I set in our sessions; he had his own agenda. The "insensitive" piece was beginning to make sense. In our fourth session, I assigned the Life Line. Three years later, he completed the task.

For hour after hour, week after week, I sat with Bob as he reviewed the events of his life. He compiled his life line on his computer, using those long sheets of paper that most computers can accommodate. He would bring in one or two sheets at a time, and as we drew near the end of the last page, he'd bring in a couple more pages.

His ability to recall the minute details of his life was incredible to me. At times, staying awake was my greatest challenge. At other times, I was riveted to my chair in rapt attention. As time went by, he became more and more comfortable with the process and with our relationship. As that happened, he began going back to times we had already covered, to tell me something he had "forgotten" to mention. Those forgotten stories were about the really painful experiences in his life, and he had a lot of them.

For 3 years, I participated in Bob's personalized therapy regime, designed and implemented by the client. I was pretty much through after the fourth session, when I assigned the Life Line. In our final sessions, Bob talked about how much the process had meant to him. No one had ever taken such an interest in him. No one had ever listened to the story of his life. We wept. Thank God, for once in my life, I had the sense to keep my mouth shut and let Bob do things his way. I could never have planned such a positive experience for him myself. Four months after our work together was completed, Bob died of a heart attack.

Family Memories

This tool appeared in *Group Exercises for Adolescents: A Manual for Therapists*. I have always used it in individual therapy as well as in group work for all ages. It tends to elicit material and emotions that do not come up in the course of discussion.

Instructions

Give your client a large sheet of drawing paper and colored markers. Tell him or her to divide the paper in half with a line down the middle. On one half of the paper, ask your client to draw a happy family memory, a scene from childhood when things were good. On the other half, ask him or her to draw an unhappy family memory, a scene from childhood when things were bad. The time in childhood does not matter; a memory from any age is fine. Whatever comes to mind will work.

I like to use large paper with a line down the middle rather than two sheets of paper. The sight of both a positive and a negative experience is an excellent nonverbal reminder to clients that both good and bad things happened in the family of their childhood.

Although clients sometimes complain about drawing (usually because they are embarrassed by their lack of artistic ability), reassure them that artistic ability will not be evaluated, nor is it the point. The point is to provide an opportunity for our clients to express themselves in a way that is different from the speaking or writing mode, and to maybe learn something new in the process.

The scenes that pop into consciousness may be unexpected. Encourage your client to go with the first thing that pops into his or her head if possible, without censoring initial images in search of more "appropriate" memories.

I like to do this exercise in session rather than as homework, although it would certainly work just fine to have your clients take the assignment home. I have found that clients will clean things up a bit if they do this at home. In the office, they seem to work quickly and more spontaneously. Also, I think it is nice for our clients to experience our silent attention while they work. I try to be careful not to peer over their shoulder or stare at them while they work. I imagine myself like a good parent, quietly available.

When they finish the drawing, it's time to process the work by asking them to explain the scenes depicted. You will get a lot of information about childhood issues and family dynamics from this simple tool. When you explore the drawings, your clients may discover new insights as well.

Materials

- A large sheet of drawing paper
- Colored markers

Practice Examples

Usually, but not always, the majority of material for therapy is elicited by the negative family memory. However, the positive scene is more revealing for some clients.

A Positive Family Memory

This story is from my days as a psychiatric nurse working on an adult inpatient unit at a hospital. The patient, Kenny, was a young man with myriad problems, including a history of drug abuse and several suicide attempts. His Axis I diagnosis was major depression; Axis II was dependent personality disorder.

His family of origin was very dysfunctional. His stepfather was an alcoholic, and his mother was schizophrenic. He had what seemed like a vast array of siblings, stepsiblings, and half siblings from a variety of parents, some living in the home, others living here and there with their other parent. The climate of the household was unpredictable, to say the least. Routine, stability, consistency, and structure were foreign to this family. Although Kenny made episodic attempts to live on his own, he always seemed to wind up moving back home.

Now in his early 20s, Kenny was one of those unfortunate people who enter and leave mental facilities on a regular basis. "Kenny's back," the nurse on the admitting shift would report, and those of us on the oncoming shift would shake our collective heads sadly.

But Kenny was likable. He had an endearing quality that was enough to keep our frustration at bay. As needy as he was, he did not want to be; independence eluded him like an errant child.

Late one night, he couldn't sleep, so we were talking in the day room. I retrieved a large sheet of paper and some markers from the supply closet and asked him to draw a happy family memory and an unhappy family memory. He worked away as I filled out charts. When he was finished, we were both amazed. Kenny had a happy family memory that looked like anyone else's. He had drawn his family at Christmas. There was a Christmas tree with presents under it. It was a Christmas when his biological father and mother were together. Brothers and sisters and the family pets, a dog and a cat, were in the picture. Huge smiles filled the circles that were the faces of what could have been any ordinary, middle-class family. Kenny talked to me about other positive memories, about learning to ride a bike one summer with his father's help and swimming at the river with his older brother. If only for a while, Kenny was in touch with some memories of his family and his childhood that he could think of as normal and even as good. If we can facilitate the capture of such comforting material, then we have given our patients a gift indeed. Catch and release isn't just for fishing.

Unhappy Family Memories

Agneta sought therapy when her second marriage began to fall apart. The tall, attractive real estate broker had a 17-year-old daughter and a 12-year-old son from a previous marriage. She and her husband, a commercial contractor, had been married for 7 years.

She met her first husband, the father of her children, in Sweden. He was traveling in Europe the summer after graduating from college. Agneta, a second-generation American, was visiting her grandparents in Sweden. They married 2 years later; the marriage lasted 8 years. The cause of the breakup was that her husband was having an affair.

Now, she suspected her current husband was cheating. She had no real evidence of that, but he was increasingly disinterested in her and preoccupied in general. He claimed it was business demands; she didn't believe him.

Her husband did not know she was in therapy at this point, although we talked about marital counseling as a goal for the future. She felt certain he would balk at the prospect of counseling when he denied an affair and chided Agneta for her suspicions. He also told her that he refused to get upset anymore because no matter what he did, it would never be enough; she would never really trust him.

This situation is like so many we encounter in therapy. As Agneta's therapist, I did not know the real situation. Was she right, and her husband was being unfaithful? If he was, why would two husbands stray? Was it something about her? Was she difficult, hard to live with? Or did she simply choose two men who were unwilling or unable to commit to one woman? If she was wrong and her husband was telling her the truth, then why couldn't she trust him? Was it because he was so poor at communicating his affection for her that she had no reason to believe him? Did he treat her poorly? Could it be that she was still so wounded from the betrayal in her first marriage that she could not trust any man? If she is mistrusting of men, is she mistrusting only of men, or of people in general? If she is mistrusting of men, why? If she finds it difficult to trust in general, why?

When it is hard to size up the real issues, it's nice to have a tool or two to pull out of your toolbox. Wanting to know more about her family of origin, I reached for the Family Memories exercise.

Her unhappy family memory revealed a lot. Agneta described it as "the worst thing that ever happened to me." She drew a picture of a stick figure standing on the world as a globe. The female figure is standing someplace in Europe (depicted by the shape of the continent) and is reaching up to the sky. In the sky overhead, an airplane is flying by. Agneta explained that when she was 7 or 8 years old, her parents took her to Sweden to spend the summer with her grandparents. She did not know her grandparents well because they lived so far away. She had grown up with images of her grandparents as represented by her parents. They told her that her grandparents were nice old people who lived across the ocean in a faraway land where everyone spoke another language. Now, her parents were leaving her in this strange land with the legendary grandparents who were essentially strangers to the little girl. She remembered seeing her parents off at the airport when they left and how it felt to watch as the giant silver plane rose into the sky and disappeared. In her mind, her parents were disappearing forever; they would never be back. All summer long, she looked longingly at every plane that went overhead, wondering if it might be the plane carrying her parents back to her.

I did not get the complete picture of Agneta's situation with this one exercise—not by a long shot—but now I could see that a profound fear of abandonment was one of the issues to address. It was a good place to start and, in the end, was the defining element. Agneta began to learn about issues of abandonment in general, and her own specifically. She also came to understand that her adult fears of abandonment were often exaggerated and unrealistic. As she began to understand herself better, she was able to relax her grip on the people in her life who meant the most, her husband in particular. As Agneta changed, her husband changed in response, and the marriage relationship improved.

I am always amazed at the strength of people who overcome devastating events that occurred early in their lives. At a time when the adults in their lives are supposed to be loving and protecting their children, really awful things happen. It has been difficult enough for me to maintain a sense of self-worth and confidence, although I was blessed with a happy and secure childhood. I cannot imagine what it must be like for so many of our clients, who, instead of being supported and cherished, were painfully wounded by the very ones upon whom they depended. Such was the case with my client Nichole.

Nichole was a registered nurse working in a local hospital. As with many caregivers, one way Nichole tried to heal her own unmet dependency needs was by serving others. (See "The Dribble Theory of Happiness," p. 189.) Nichole found herself in one emotionally abusive relationship after the other. She was well aware of the pattern but seemed unable to change it. She was attracted to men who needed her care, either physically or emotionally or both. They were neither as intelligent nor as successful as she was. In each case, the men slowly but surely became demanding and demeaning. Nichole would remain in the relationship long after it was clear that she should get out. She came to therapy shortly after a nasty breakup with her third tumultuous relationship. Nichole was an African American; for the most part, the men in her life had been white.

Nichole had been in therapy with me for about a month when I asked her to do the Family Memories exercise. Preceding sessions had dealt with the fallout from her recent breakup. When she drew her unhappy memory, an important dynamic became clear.

Her unhappy family memory showed a large open mouth at the top left corner of the page. The curled lips and visible tongue depicted anger or disdain. Lines coming from the mouth spread out in all directions. At the opposite lower corner was a small female figure, tiny in comparison to the snarling mouth above. Nichole explained that the mouth represented her mother. She said that her mother hated everything about her that was black. Nichole's mother was a light-skinned African American. Nichole, like her father, was much darker and had more traditional African features. Her parents had a rocky relationship, and finally, her father deserted the family, leaving her mother in charge of five young children. Nichole said her mother hated her daughter's flared nostrils, the shape of her heels, literally every feature that identified her as an African American.

The tiny person sketched in the opposite corner was Nichole. Her drawing spoke volumes. Small, helpless, unworthy, almost invisible, the tiny little girl was barely on the page. Nichole chose white men for a complex set of reasons, but suddenly, it was clear that one of them had to do with a sense of wrongness about her identity as a black woman. She had also spent a lifetime tolerating abuse from a significant person in her life (her mother). When the men she chose became abusive, she knew how to tolerate it; she had been doing it all her life.

That session marked the beginning of much more, and much better therapy. The family memories tool provided a way for Nichole to teach me about her experience. I am a white woman. My client needed a way to share an experience with me that I not only have never had, but also do not even have a frame of reference for. However, I do know what it feels like to be demeaned, discounted, and despised, so I could be more fully empathic with her. The family memories exercise was a bonding event, like glue, for Nichole and me.

Every Now and Zen
Meditation and Mindfulness for the Beginner

In my work as a college chaplain and a therapist, I have learned the value of meditation both for myself and for my clients. There have been times in my life that discipline prevailed and I meditated on a regular basis. Other times, I did not practice meditation at all. Then, I began using a method that seemed a good balance between the demands of regular meditation and no meditation.

These days, the complexities of life infect us all. No one seems to escape the social, emotional, and economic pressures of our fast-paced culture. Meditation is a bridge that offers an escape from external demands and provides a passageway into the more peaceful territory of matters internal and eternal. I can't think of anyone (who is not psychotic) who would not benefit from meditation.

I have been teaching this model to my clients for about 4 years, and it seems to provide a good basic beginning to the practice of this ancient art. The form offered here is based on Zen Buddhist techniques. I think therapists should have this tool for their own use, and to lend to clients. Mastering its use means that you can pull it out of your toolbox every now and then.

Instructions

The following instructions are written just as I say them to my clients; you will have your own way of expressing the material.

Begin by getting as comfortable as you can. It seems that most people relax best with both feet on the floor, and with their hands in their lap. You might want to try that, or you may have a position that is better for you. [Pause.]

It is easier to meditate with your eyes closed, so that you can cut out the visual stimuli around you. So, if you are comfortable doing so, close your eyes now.

Notice your body. Get all of your body back into itself. Put your legs into your legs. [Pause.] Put your trunk into itself. [Pause.] Put your arms and hands inside your arms and hands where they belong. [Pause.] And get your head back into your head. [Pause.]

Notice the weight of your body; pay attention to the weight of your feet on the floor. [Pause.] Now pay attention to your legs and notice how heavy they feel. [Pause.] Notice your pelvis and buttocks and the small of your back. Allow that whole area to just sink into the sofa/couch/chair. [Pause.] Feel the weight of your back against the cushion. [Pause.] Notice the weight of your head on your torso (or as it rests against the cushion). [Pause.]

Now, pay attention to your breathing. Don't try to change or alter the way you are breathing, just pay attention. [Longer pause.]

Our brothers and sisters in the East say that we in the West are not happy because we are not present in the moment. They say that we are preoccupied with our future and held captive by our past, so we miss the present moment. Being present in the moment is also called *mindfulness*. Right now, we are practicing mindfulness, the art of being present in the moment.

They also say that we in the West think too much. We are always thinking, thinking, thinking. . . . Our thoughts are all over the place. . . . So, as a way to contain and control your thinking right now, try this: As you are breathing in, say (to yourself, in your mind) "I am breathing in." And when you are breathing out, say (to yourself, in your mind) "I am breathing out." Try that. [Pause long enough that several breath cycles occur.]

Now, your thoughts are focused, but there are still many words in your thoughts. This time, when you breathe, try this: As you are breathing in, say (to yourself, in your mind) "In," and when you are breathing out, say (to yourself, in your mind) "Out." [Pause long enough that several breath cycles occur.]

This time, see if you can let go of the words "in" and "out," and just be with your breathing; try not to use words. [Pause quite a while here so that your client can experience success, which you hope will occur right at first, then probable failure as thoughts creep back in.]

As you see, it is not easy to clear your mind of random thoughts. Just remember that when random thoughts show up, you can gently dismiss them. You can also go back to the "in" and "out" words to get back on track.

This is a reasonable stopping point. Encourage your client to practice what was just learned on a regular basis. However, there may be a more helpful path for some people. You need to know your client's spiritual/religious orientation. Is your client Jewish? Christian? Muslim? Other? Consider using these next instructions if your client sees him- or herself as a spiritual/religious person.

> You might want to create a mantra or chant for yourself, a word or phrase that connects you to your deepest spiritual resource. The choice of this word or words should be yours. I will give you some ideas that may be helpful.

- If your client is Jewish: As you breathe in, say "Be with me," and as you breathe out, say "O God." Or, you might try "Give thanks to God" as you inhale, and "For God is good" as you exhale.

- If your client is Christian: As you breathe in, say "Be near me," and as you breathe out, say "Lord Jesus." Or, you could try "Come" as you inhale, and "Holy Spirit" as you exhale. Or, perhaps "Holy and Gracious" on the inhale, and "God, three in one" on the exhale.

- If your client is Muslim: As you breathe in, say "I strive for righteousness," and as you breathe out, say "In the sight of Allah."

- If your client is "Other," such as a member of a Twelve-Step Program, and uses the group consciousness as his or her Higher Power: As you breathe in, say "The power of the group," and as you breathe out, say "protects and informs me." Or, you might try "I am connected with love" as you inhale, and "to a supportive community" as you exhale.

It is helpful to have some more conversation about how meditation and mindfulness (being present in the moment) has practical, everyday applications. I use a story about Thich Nhat Hanh, the Buddhist monk from Vietnam who achieved worldwide recognition for his role in the Paris Peace Talks and was nominated for a Nobel Peace Prize. The story I tell my clients is about this remarkable man when he was a little boy. The 4-year-old boy looked forward to his mother's trips to the market because it meant that a delightful treat was in store for him. She always brought back a cookie. The future monk would take his treasure outside, where he would sit in the front yard and enjoy the delicacy. Slowly, bit by bit, he ate the cherished cookie. As he savored each small nibble, he noticed his environment. He paid attention to all that was around him, the smell of the earth, the beauty of the sky, the way the sunlight played on the bamboo thicket nearby. It took the little boy 45 minutes to eat his cookie. He was happy.

After telling the story, I ask my clients how long it took them to eat their most recent meal. Sometimes, I ask them what they ate. The usual response is that it took only a few minutes to eat breakfast or lunch, and often, they cannot recall what they had to eat. The point has been made. Enjoyment of food and the ritual of a meal were lost because the person was not present in the moment.

Then, I point out that although there are a number of issues that brought them to therapy, at this moment, things are good. We are having a pleasant conversation, the client is learning something new, neither of us is sick, we are both relatively comfortable in our seats, and so on. The peace and comfort of the moment is available to us, but we don't always seem able to appreciate it.

Practice Example

I am using my own story, instead of a client's, to illustrate a way to plug this meditation and mindfulness technique into a busy life.

Stoplights used to be my enemy. Because I am bivocational, I have two offices; they are across town from each other, of course. It often seems that no matter what I want, it is in the other office. On top of that, I am persistently late; to meetings, to appointments, to lunch dates, you name it. So, I'm constantly driving across town in a dead heat with very little time to spare. I had about a zillion ways to avoid stoplights, but in spite of my best efforts and most cunning plans, there is no way to miss them all. Inevitably, the dreaded red light would cross my path. When it did, I agonized over every second that went by while I white-knuckled the steering wheel and ground my teeth.

When I learned to meditate and practice mindfulness at stoplights, my relationship with them changed completely. It occurred to me that there were free minutes available when I was in traffic waiting for a light to turn green. I started using a shortened version of the meditation technique described. I had practiced the technique long enough that I could quickly become mindful of my breathing. I also discovered that I could focus on my body, and the weight of it sitting there in the car, very quickly as well; therefore, relaxation could be achieved in no time. (Of course, I did not close my eyes in the middle of traffic!) Then, I would begin my mantra or chant. That's all there is to it! I discovered this golden opportunity to escape whatever frantic concerns I was dwelling on by meditating at stoplights. I cannot say that I am never impatient at stoplights anymore, or that I am always grateful when the light turns red.

I'm only saying that it is much better now. I am less apt to be anxious, and I feel happier if I remember to meditate.

Suggested Reading

Nhat Hahn, T. (1992). *Peace is every step: The path of mindfulness in everyday life.* New York: Bantam.

Journaling 101

When I begin therapy with a new client, I usually talk to him or her about journaling. Sometimes, journaling becomes a major focus of therapy; clients write in their journals between appointments and bring them to session each time. A format for therapy evolves as we process the material together. Other times, the client's journal is a very occasional source of material for work in session. He or she may bring the journal only when it seems important to share a particular entry with me. Of course, there are those people who just do not like to write. If that is the case, I let it go, and journaling is not a part of the therapy.

I think a discussion of journaling, and an explanation of the benefits of journaling, is important even if it does not become part of the therapy experience. At least you have introduced your client to an important resource that can be used at any time, whether or not the person is in therapy.

Instructions

The following is an example of what I might say to my own clients.

I want to tell you about journaling because it is an important and effective tool for self-discovery and personal growth. If you just hate to write, this probably won't work for you, but if you enjoy at least some writing, such as writing letters or composing e-mail messages, you might like journaling.

Journaling is making written entries into a notebook or your computer to record your thoughts and feelings about life on a regular basis. A journal is not like a diary in that there is no demand for daily entries. When people think of writing in a diary, often they feel they must make a daily entry or else fail in some way. Therefore, feelings of pressure, commitment, success, and failure may be associated with diaries. In personal journaling, entries are made only when the writer has something to express and wishes to write it down. Some people journal every day to be sure, but a successful journal may be a book of quite sporadic entries.

Some of my clients who journal use a spiral notebook with lined pages; others buy lovely cloth-covered or hardbound journals with blank pages. A few of my clients prefer to journal on their computers. What you choose to use is up to you. You should feel secure in your ability to conceal your journal from everyone. Journaling is a private affair.

The reason journaling is so important is that it helps you recognize and own your feelings. When you have thoughts and feelings about people, situations, events, or beliefs in your mind, they sort of float around in an amorphous fog. But when you write down those thoughts and feelings, you are forced to identify and organize them. When you commit that material to the written word, ownership is enhanced. It is not unusual for a person who is journaling to suddenly realize, "Oh! That's how I feel!" There's also something to be said about just getting that stuff out of your body. Catharsis, or the act of getting rid of something by expressing it, has long been known to have healing properties in and of itself.

A second step in ownership occurs when you share that material with another person—me, your therapist. My clients read their journal entries to me; that way, not only do you get to hear your own thoughts once again, but you also take the next step of sharing them. Then, you and I will talk about what you have written, as we need to.

Practice Examples

Melanie was married to a professional musician who was a portrait of the negative stereotype. He was irresponsible, unavailable, and self-consumed. He expected Melanie to forgive him all of that because he was, after all, an artist. It was her job to make his life as easy as possible so that he could devote his full attention to his work. Meanwhile, they had three young children, and Melanie worked full-time; or, as she said, "Actually, I have four children, counting Steve" (her husband).

By the time she entered therapy, she had lost all respect for her "adolescent husband," as she called him. She had been completely defeated in her every effort to improve their relationship and his parenting (or nonparenting). Exhausted, physically ill with chronic migraines, and definitely out of love with her husband, she was at her wit's end.

The complicating piece for her was that she was devout in her religious convictions, and her church was contemptuous of divorce. It was simply not allowed. It was clear at the outset that the only way Melanie could escape the trap of a debilitating marriage was to give herself permission to unlock the cage; no one else could do it for her.

We discussed journaling early in therapy, and she liked the idea. Although she had never kept a diary nor recorded her thoughts or feelings on paper since a creative writing class back in college, she was intrigued. Soon, I became privy to the war that waged within her.

I felt it was my responsibility to hold up the vision of leaving her husband as a reasonable choice. Because I am a religious person myself, she had to deal with the reality of my history. I am a chaplain, I am divorced, I am remarried, I am happy, and I am free. I held the vision, and she did the work.

Her journal entries read like a tale of spiritual warfare. Her desire for freedom fought with her conviction of commitment. The God of her understanding battled with another God, a Force that was more interested in setting her free than in keeping her captive.

She had a rich and wonderful dialogue with herself. "Melanie," she would read to me from her journal, "Why don't you save yourself and your children? This marriage is destroying you! Your children don't really have a father anyway. Why do you continue to think that something horrible will happen if you leave him? Steve will be fine. Steve is always fine. How can you be so worried about a man who treats you with such indifference?"

Answering herself, she would say, "Because, you selfish woman, there is always hope. God promises that all things work together for good for his people. This is a test. If you stay true to the promises you made to Steve, God will honor those promises and Steve will change."

Her alter ego would again respond, "Steve will change! Have you lost your mind? Not in 15 years has Steve changed! How long do you have to wait?"

She did lots of other work in therapy along with her private journaling, of course. We talked about her family of origin, the roots of her faith, the history of her marriage to Steve, her children, and so on, but through it all, there was the journaling, a record of her struggle and eventual transformation. (Yes, she left him.)

Karen began therapy with me upon her release from hospitalization in a psychiatric facility. Hospitalization occurred when her husband discovered her in a semiconscious state from an overdose of her psychotropic medication. Karen's records from the hospital indicated diagnoses of major depression, posttraumatic stress disorder, and borderline personality disorder. The progress notes revealed a difficult hospitalization with numerous episodes of acting-out behaviors, including cutting on herself with a safety pin that she smuggled into the unit, returning drunk from a pass, and running away on a unit out-trip, along with a variety of infringements of unit rules and regulations.

In our early sessions together, she was withdrawn and almost recalcitrant, peeking at me suspiciously from under her ball cap. It was clear that she saw me as another authority figure with whom to wrestle. However, in spite of herself, the desire to know me and be known by me was the stronger suit and won out over time.

I learned that her alcoholic father had sexually abused her from age 12 through age 17, at which time she left home. Not long after she escaped, he shot and killed himself. A complicated mix of emotions about the father she both hated and adored, wished dead and missed, tortured her.

She chose a husband very like her father. They had two children, a boy, 14, and a girl, 12. It was no accident that her repressed issues roared to the surface when her children became the age she was at the time of her abuse.

The discovery that Karen all but missed the experience of being a teenager was a precious find. A number of things made sense in light of her lost adolescence, including her shenanigans during hospitalization and her "gamey" behavior with me. So, we began to find ways to recapture those lost years, to reclaim her adolescence, so to speak, with the goal of healing what we could of the past, and helping her grow into a healthy adult woman.

Instead of introducing the journaling process as I usually do, I suggested that maybe she should keep a diary, as young girls are wont to do. The notion captured her imagination, but in her Karen-like way, she put her own twist on it.

Over the next 5 years, Karen wrote me letters on a regular basis. She occasionally sent them in the mail, but mostly she brought them to session. The letters were a record of her reactions to events around her, memories of past trauma, questions about life and love, and reflections about her take on herself. It was journaling, to be sure, even though each entry began and ended like a letter to her therapist.

For a long time, her letters sounded like the letters of a crazy teenager. She drove too fast, tried every illegal drug on the planet, was irresponsible, and used bad judgment. For example, in her work, Karen did quite a bit of traveling; she would drive on long trips and write letters as she sped down the highway!

Occasionally, reading her lengthy tomes took most of the session, but it was important work; a way to share deeply held fears and affections. Somehow, reading her letters was safer than articulating spontaneously; it was less of a threat. She would read and I would honor the work, and she would read and I would honor the work. . . .

Sometimes, we went through periods when she did not journal, and those were times of good work, too. But when the going got tough, like when the horrible dreams started again, or when someone she thought was a friend betrayed her, or when she found herself teetering on the brink of the abyss once again (her depression), the letters would start.

Karen is doing well; I haven't seen her for several months now. It is our sixth year of therapy. Isn't adolescence about 6 years?

Kim's father was an enigma in her life. He had been very successful in his profession as a surgeon. He was an intelligent, driven, powerful man, but not always emotionally available to his daughter. I came to know him through her eyes in therapy.

Kim entered therapy at age 48 when fibromyalgia and chronic fatigue syndrome threatened her ability to continue working. She had been living with an aching body and fairly constant fatigue for 3 years. She had curtailed most of the activities of her life in an attempt to conserve her resources so that she could continue her work as the owner of a travel agency. Kim was happily married to her husband of 24 years. They had two children, both grown and out of the home.

She was under the care of a medical doctor specializing in arthritis and related disorders, belonged to a fibromyalgia support group, consulted regularly with a nutritionist, and took yoga classes. She was well-read on both fibromyalgia and chronic fatigue, and she frequented the Internet to stay current on new research. She decided to try individual therapy with the hope that there might be something in the process that would, if nothing else, help her cope with her lack of progress.

We started exploring her relationship with her father early in therapy. He was a daunting figure, a large man with the huge, weathered hands of a farmer. Strangers were always surprised to learn of his real occupation. He was an outdoorsman who loved his native Minnesota and was an accomplished hunter and fisherman. His medical practice was in an urban setting, but he owned a log cabin on a nearby lake where the family spent most of their summers when Kim was growing up. Her father treasured his retreat and furnished it lavishly with authentic period pieces and Native works of art.

Kim was obliged to adore her father from afar. Although her two brothers caught his attention on occasion, she was merely a guest, a relative. He taught the boys to hunt and fish and kept a wary eye on their athletic and academic progress. But Kim was mostly ignored, an invisible presence. The reality of her relative unimportance to him was not felt as long as her mother was alive. The two women in the family were very close. But when her mother died 6 years ago and her father became her only parent, she was confronted with the reality of their relationship.

Now, with her illness pushing her into all of the unexplored territory of her life, it was time to confront the impact of her relationship with her father.

Her father's parsimony of attention and affection on the emotional level was duplicated on the material level as well; a dark presence permeated his character. Although quite wealthy, he would not or could not share his money, even with his children. Whereas other parents of similar fortune gave their children gifts of fine art, furniture, cars, or equipment, he only loaned these things, and occasionally, years later, he would collect the painting, oriental rug, chair, or chain saw that he had loaned so long ago. He had hoarded things for as long as Kim could remember. Food, weapons, gasoline, and other emergency supplies were always on hand in the basement. The collecting and hoarding behaviors seemed related to Kim; it was as if he needed to have things around him in order to feel safe or comfortable.

He collected fine art, fine wine, hunting and fishing equipment, coins, and vehicles (he always had at least four cars and a boat or two). Over the years, there were many times and many ways that Kim's father could have helped his children financially, but he never did.

I listened to all her stories, pulled a nail out of my toolbox at an important juncture for a little repair (see "They Didn't Mean To . . ." p. 187), and then moved on to Journaling 101. When I introduced Kim to journaling, I expected her to write about her conflicted feelings about her father, as most people do in the journaling process. But she took the assignment in a whole new direction. She decided that if she wanted to improve her relationship with her father, now age 75, she was the one who had to do the changing, not him. Focusing on the negative aspects of their relationship would not bring the peace she sought. So, she bought a notebook and began writing all the positive things she could think of about her father. She wrote about the kind-hearted things he had done over the years, about his commendable behaviors, and about all of his positive attributes. She recorded all the good memories she had of him. When she told her brother what she was doing, he asked if he could write in her journal, too; then, her children asked if they could record what they loved about their grandfather. The journal became a family project, a decision to honor a complicated individual who was so important to all of them. In the process, Kim's feelings about her father changed, and their relationship improved.

Favorite Fairy Tales

Fairy tales are excellent tools to use in therapy. If you are like me, thinking that we put away the influence of fairy tales along with the rest of our childhood toys, think again. These mythical messages can have a defining influence on how a person views self, gender, and even life in general. Consider using this tool if you are working with a client who is searching for the answer to the question "Who am I, and why do I do what I do?"

Fairy tales serve as good examples of how images beyond family and personal experience play an important role in shaping our personalities and our perceptions of the world. They can be included in the important cultural consciousness that affects our development as human beings. Sometimes, you will be able to enlighten clients by helping them see that, on some level, they have bought into a mythical notion that is a pretty far cry from reality. Then you can say, "No wonder you did such-and-such! It makes perfect sense to have reacted in that way when, way down deep inside, you believed (whatever it was from some fairy tale)!" That is an empowering statement for clients to hear. It helps them feel less crazy when they can see that cultural influences are at work, and they are not operating out of some isolated, sick place inside their own minds.

Instructions

I like to do this as a writing exercise because I hope that clients will allow the story to hang around in their thoughts for a few days, mulling over the characters and just "being with" the images it evokes; therefore, I assign it as homework. I have done this right in session on occasion when it seemed the best option, but I prefer using it as homework.

Tell your clients that their assignment is to write about their favorite fairy tale. They need to answer the following questions: (a) What is the story, and why am I drawn to it? (b) To which character am I drawn in this story, and why? and (c) Has this story played out in my life?

For some, the favorite fairy tale will jump into their minds at once. Others may indicate that they don't have a favorite. If that is the case, give them a little more help. Suggest that there is probably one or two that they find more interesting than others. They may never have consciously designated a favorite, but they may just like the story or characters in one tale better than in others. Encourage them to think about it. I have a whole bookshelf full of fairy tales that I have collected over the years, and I have several anthologies. I let my clients peruse my collection and take some home if they wish.

I have learned over the years to give the fairy tale definition a wide berth. I have found that baby boomers are familiar with a wide variety of classic fairy tales, but people from subsequent generations have a different frame. Some know only the classic fairy tales that have been animated as movies, and others think of *Star Wars* or television creations as fairy tales. That's fine. The vehicle doesn't matter; it's the story that counts. If *The Little Engine That Could* was a favorite childhood book, I bet there's something in the tale that will be relevant in therapy.

Ask your clients to bring their homework to the next session. When they do, ask them to read to you what they have written. (Whenever clients do written work, whether they journal or are working on an assignment like this one, I ask them to read what they have written to me. This not only ensures that both of you are actively sharing the material, but also adds another opportunity for clients to own their thoughts and feelings more deeply.)

Some clients will give you a blank look in response to your instructions. They can't think of any fairy tales, much less a favorite one. In that case, talk to them about your favorite childhood stories. You might ask them to reflect upon stories that their mother or father read to them when they were little. If they maintain that they have no stories and no one read to them, you have a therapy issue; grist for the mill. Why don't they have stories? Why didn't anyone read to them? You have provided an opportunity for conversation that may not have emerged otherwise, and you may learn as much from that as you would have with the exercise.

Practice Examples

"Sleeping Beauty," "Snow White," and "Cinderella" are often chosen as favorites. I think of them as a trilogy, three tales with similar patterns. I have had so many women with similar issues choose one of these, that instead of presenting one client's experience, I think it is more helpful to offer the pattern that tends to emerge.

Clients who choose one of these are usually disappointed in their spouse/partner. Life with him is not at all like they had imagined. They were so sure they had found the prince. He was prince-like in today's terms: wealthy, intelligent, bright future, from a good family. He had power as well. He might be a doctor, a lawyer, a judge, a politician, or some other public figure. He was all they ever wanted; they were so lucky to have been chosen. Connection to this all-important male was all that was needed. Hitching one's wagon to a star ensured happiness ever after. But somewhere along the line, something went wrong. The heir to the throne turned out to be an addict, perhaps—alcohol, drugs, work, golf, you name it. Or maybe he was a womanizer, a tyrant, or just plain disinterested in his queen. Sometimes, the queen lived in the kingdom, but she had no access to its riches (literal riches; money).

These women will tell you how hard they tried; they followed all the rules. The Cinderellas dutifully cleaned and swept and took care of relatives, the Snow Whites served their men cheerfully, and the Sleeping Beauties exercised and dieted and "kept themselves up." And they waited. They tried and they waited. But the king did not change.

Passivity is often an issue with these women, and one can see why. If their heroines followed the rules, were nice to everyone, and looked good, they got the golden key. Why not them? The importance of independence and self-reliance is not the theme of these fairy tales.

Well, I do love fairy tales. The magic and mystery are wonderful, and the trials and tribulations heart-rending. I hope we'll always have them around. But there are some harmful messages in them at times, certainly for women. Some of them I've mentioned, but there are more. You don't hear much about wicked stepfathers or evil kings; I bet there are more witches than there are goblins or warlocks.

Of course, men don't have it so easy either. You don't much count in the fairy tale scheme of things if you are not a rich, handsome prince. You can be poor and ugly and clever at first, but unless you are clever enough to become a prince before it's all over, never mind.

These ideas have been documented and researched by scholars who are certainly more informed than I am. There is much more to say than what I'm offering here. But I don't think you have to be afraid to try this exercise with clients just because you have never had a course in women's studies. Your clients will teach you a lot. Just offer them a way to do it.

Martin's wife discovered that he was having an affair. She came to see me the first time by herself. She was terribly upset, hurt, and angry, but also determined to fight for her marriage. She felt sure that her husband would agree to counseling, which he did. After 2 months of marital therapy, the crisis of the affair was over. Martin gradually broke away from the other woman and recommitted to his wife. Then, he decided to do some individual therapy with me in addition to the marital work.

Martin was an attractive, middle-aged corporate type who knew how to dress for success. His meticulous grooming was a metaphor for other aspects of his persona. Martin was self-contained, the sort of person who had the capacity to hold back or restrain his emotions—so much so that one never really knew what he was feeling, not even him. He was adept at articulating his thoughts, but when it came to his feelings, he was rendered mute. Martin lived a carefully constructed life as well. Every move was calculated and planned in advance. His climb up the career ladder had the organization and strategy of a well-planned football play. He was also a triathlete who ground through workout regimes like a machine. But his real passion was rock climbing—mountains, cliffs, sheer walls, you name it. Control and discipline were the watchwords of his life. No one was more surprised at his extramarital tryst than Martin himself.

I felt a sense of dread every time he was scheduled for therapy. When he was in the office, I confronted the glass floor instead of the glass ceiling. You could only go down so far. Our conversations were about as deep as the water in a birdbath. He was charming, nice, and oh, so cooperative. But in terms of real presence, he might as well have been at a cocktail party as in his therapist's office.

The talk-therapy thing just was not working, and the sessions were agony for me (and probably for him as well, but then that would mean he was feeling something, and I wasn't sure of that). I reached into my toolbox for something. A drill? Jackhammer? How about a saw? In an attempt to get through that floor, I decided to try an unlikely device, the fairy tale exercise.

His reaction to my fairy tale idea made me feel silly, like a little girl who just invited a grown-up to a tea party. But he was polite and went along with me in spite of the unmistakable look on his face.

In our next session, he read his assignment to me. He could not remember the name of the story he loved as a child, but he remembered the story. It was about a little boy and a monster. The little boy was dreadfully afraid of the monster, but ends up befriending him. The boy and the scary monster become great pals.

Martin could not tell me what the monster represented. He identified strongly with the boy, however, and remembered that he was comforted hearing the story as a child. Growing up, he thought about the tale on occasion and he would be comforted again.

I asked Martin if it was possible that the monster represented fear; maybe a particular fear, or perhaps fear in general. Yes, he liked that idea. I asked if he could talk about that a little.

Thus began the story of Mr. Corporate America's fear. The first image that came to his mind was a confrontation with his football coach when he was in the ninth grade. He was short and stout, 5'4" and 130 pounds. His small stature did not diminish his love for football. He loved not only the game itself, but also what football represented, a badge of acceptance. The guys who played football were automatically inducted into the Hall of Masculinity.

Martin's sense of acceptability as an adequate male was compromised not only by his physique, but also by his family's status in the community. His parents were rural folk, poor and uneducated by the standards of his urban peers. His girlfriend's father owned a furniture store, and his best friend's dad was a pharmacist. Martin's dad milked cows, fixed fences, and worked at the feed store. The issue of class was as strongly entrenched in the small Kansas town as the issue of caste was in premodern India. Playing football was the override button for questions of class and masculinity. If you played football, and played well, all other sins were forgiven. Martin would play.

The season had already started, and Martin was a freshman scrub. Freshman scrubs were those boys who were not good enough to make the varsity. The scrubs were used as guinea pigs to play against the middle school team, which consisted of the best of the seventh- and eighth-grade players. Among those middle schoolers was one Sammy Brown, a 245-pound monolith who ruled the field and was the reason the team was undefeated. Nobody could stop Sammy; he plowed through the line of scrimmage every play. It was as if the linemen were ghosts, transparent and formless. They fell from his charging frame like weightless specters. Only Martin and two other equally terrorized, undersized defensive backs remained between Sammy and the goal post. Martin felt not only the ball of fear in his gut, but also the humiliation and inadequacy that defined him in the first place as he confronted the giant foe. As much as he longed for the courage to throw caution to the wind and hurl himself into the giant's path, the instinct of self-preservation won out and Sammy, undaunted, crossed the goal line.

On this particular day, the coach, joined by his snickering staff, was laughing his ass off. Basically, the coaching staff was gleeful, and the scrubs were the objects of their mirth. "You bunch of sissies!" the coach roared, still laughing. "Are you going to let one man run over all of you?"

That was the most humiliating moment in young Martin's life, and shortly thereafter, he decided on a plan of action. He vowed not to feel anymore. That is, he would not feel anything but anger. He would not feel pain, he would not feel fear, he would not feel shame; he would feel anger, and he would feel rage. It was the only answer, and it worked.

By the time the next practice rolled around, Martin had nurtured and fed his anger into a growth spurt. Given the disparity in size, weight, and strength, he knew he could never tackle the monster-boy successfully in the usual way, so he decided on another tactic. He would go for the giant's center of gravity and knock him off balance; mighty trees are felled in the same way.

At the first opportunity, he put his anger and his plan to work. He dove for Sammy, aiming between the fullback's knee and ankle with his shoulder. He heard, rather than felt, the sound of contact, and as he slid across the ground on his stomach, he turned to look over his shoulder at the results of the impact. What he saw, he never forgot. Sammy was airborne, feet still running in midair as if his brain had not yet informed them of their whereabouts. He fell to the ground with a wheeze and a thud, the air knocked completely out of him. A cheer went up from the scrubs. Sammy was slow to get up, and Martin's life was changed forever.

Within the season, Martin advanced from freshman scrub to varsity fullback. The wiry fullback was all over the field, stinging and annoying his opponents like a pesky bee. He had only to remember the jeering coaching staff to summon the anger that fueled his aggression.

He won the admiration of both his coaches and his peers. Sammy Brown, the scary monster, became one of his teammates and best friends.

Now I knew how Martin had come to distance himself from his feelings. He did it back in the ninth grade, and it served him well. Now, however, it was disabling. It had almost cost him his marriage. He confessed that he had not felt anything for a long, long time. His obsession with extreme athletics (triathlons) and extreme sports (rock climbing) was an attempt to connect with some emotional content inside himself. When he met an enticing young woman who was attracted to him, his buried feelings exploded to the surface with a mighty force.

A direction for therapy was defined. Martin needed to give himself permission to feel again. The rest of our work together focused on connecting Martin to his emotions.

PART III

Grout, Glue, Putty, and Filler

Tools for Couples Work

The Couple's Love Story

I divorced the father of my children after 16 years of marriage and met the love of my life 3 years later. Our attraction to each other was instantaneous; our compatibility profound. Never underestimate the passion of people who feel they have another chance at love, whether they are 16, 36, or 76!

Although our relationship was secure, we only dated, deciding we would get married later, when the children left home and the dogs died. I was a therapist and he was a family court judge, and we knew about the problems of blended families.

All went well until the day it all fell apart. On that day, his teenage daughter appeared at my door, all giggles and smiles. "Want to see the car my Daddy bought me?" she said with excitement, completely innocent of the ill wind that began to blow. There, in my driveway, was a sporty, shiny new vehicle (red, of course). My problem with this otherwise fairly normal scene was that I knew nothing about the car. This man I adored and with whom I planned to share my life had not shared his plans for this major purchase with me. Now, it all was clear. He operated covertly and independently. I thought we were a team. I was not so important in his life after all; his daughter was his first priority. Our relationship was not the honest and forthright union I thought it was; it was something else indeed. It was over. I wanted out.

The man I loved had a better idea. He suggested we see a counselor. The next day, we were in the office of an able and apt therapist. Within the course of that session, I understood what I meant to this man and where I fit into his life. In the course of one session, our relationship was salvaged and my fears were put aside.

It made me a believer in the importance and effectiveness of my own work, and I have used the technique that our therapist used with us ever since.

Most of the couples with whom I work come to therapy in crisis, but this is not always the case. There are those couples who seek therapy because there is no energy or passion left between them. They would welcome a crisis if it would stir the dying embers enough to ignite a flame. Crisis or not, often the unspoken question of both partners is, "Who am I to you?" Because they may not know they are asking this question, it is up to you to create a way for the unspoken and invisible to be explored. You can do it with this technique.

Instructions

In the first or second session with a couple, after tending to the event or circumstances precipitating therapy, I like to change the pace and derail the couple's entrenched system by shifting to my own agenda. In so many words, I tell them that.

I ask them to allow me to obtain some important information that will help me in my work with them. I tell them I need to know the story of their romance. I explain that I will ask each one of them the same question. Both will have ample time to answer. The question is "How did you meet, and what was it about the other that attracted you?"

I am intentional about who begins, if it matters. For example, if one partner has trouble expressing him- or herself, I might start with the other to prime the pump. If it doesn't matter, I let them decide who begins; the way the decision is made can be a diagnostic clue. Then, I listen attentively and take notes laboriously—as if it *really* mattered (which it does). I encourage the person talking to be as specific as possible about those things that were so attractive about his or her spouse. I list every characteristic in my notes. When the person is finished, I check out my list with him or her. "Now let me be sure I have this right," I'll say, and slowly repeat the list. That way, the one listening gets to hear all those things that attracted his or her partner *twice*.

Next, turn to the other and repeat the process. I usually start by asking the question again. After checking out your list with that person, you are ready to move to the second part of the technique.

Of course, you will use your own words and do this your own way, but what I say is the following: "There is the strangest phenomenon that occurs so commonly, I feel compelled to check it out with all the couples I work with. Now this might not apply to you, but I see it all the time. The phenomenon is that the very things that attracted you to the other in the first place become the 'thorn in your side' later. Let's check it out."

Then, I'll go down each list looking for examples. Common findings are the following:

- He loved her highly verbal skills. "She always knew what to say." "She was chatty and funny and entertaining." "She understood me and put my feelings into words." Now, he's sick of her constant verbiage. He feels he never has a moment's peace. She has no idea what's going on with him because she's talking all the time.

- She was drawn to his rock-like strength. "He was so stable and secure; more of a man than the other guys I'd known." "He was solid. He had a good work ethic and was responsible." "I felt so safe with him; I knew I could lean on him." Now, he's boring. He doesn't know how to have fun. She's sick of his conservative ways. He is a tightwad, penny-pincher, stick-in-the-mud, miser, killjoy, and so on.

- She was beautiful, pretty, good-looking, gorgeous, and so on. "She looked like a model." "I was proud to have such a beautiful woman by my side." "When we walked in a room, every man in there was envious of me." "I could just look at her and melt." Now, he complains about the hours she spends on herself. She is always in the bathroom. She is never ready on time because she's still fixing her hair or makeup. He is jealous; she is too friendly with other men. Why is it that she is always flirting with guys? She must be giving them signals that she is interested in them.

- He was slightly on the "wild side," and it was exciting. "I'd never dated anyone like him." "He was such a free spirit!" "I was always Miss Good-Girl. He showed me there was another side to life." "My parents were against me dating him; that made him all the more interesting." Now, he is irresponsible. She's sick of him changing jobs all the time because he can't get along with his boss/supervisor. He is not as interested in the family as she would like; he is not a family man like her girlfriends' husbands. He acts like a child.

- She loved everything about him. "In her eyes, I could do no wrong." "She was so supportive of my ideas, my dreams, just about everything." "She made me feel special and important." "She loved me like nobody else ever had." Now he can't do anything right. She's critical of everything he does. She's sick of having to bolster his ego all the time. Where is his self-esteem? He's weak; she can't trust him to carry through on his own.

- He was sexy; there was so much chemistry between them. "I'd never felt that way about anyone!" "When he kissed me, I thought I was in heaven." "I was so physically attracted to him." "He had this physical appeal I could not resist." Now, she's sick of his constant demands for sex. She doesn't even want him to touch her because she knows where that will lead. He will never just hold her.

- He loved her energy. "She was fun and bubbly." "She was full of energy, always moving, always laughing." "She was so much fun to be around." "I loved her energy." Now, he wishes she would just back off. She overreacts to everything. She is this whirlwind that blows at him with a mighty force. She's overbearing. She's domineering.

Diagnostic Suggestions

The above list goes on and on. Your job is to discover the connection between what attracted them to each other in the first place, and how that might be playing a part in their conflict now. This technique is powerful in at least two ways: First, it takes the couple back to the best time of their relationship, a time when they were so attracted to one another that they chose to become a couple. It helps recapture those positive feelings and images that brought them together in the first place.

I try to observe the reaction of the partner who is hearing him- or herself described by the other. This observation is not an easy task because I'm also intently listening to the one talking and taking notes. However, I usually get the glimpse I need. Often, you can see the one listening visibly soften as he or she hears the other listing his or her positive characteristics. If the listening partner's expression remains rigidly fixed in disinterest, or in a scowl or some other expression of disdain, you know you've got trouble.

Sometimes, the couple will make significant eye contact as their positive statements about each other unfold. You can see the awareness of affection flow between them. If you can elicit that foundation of affection, you can build on it in subsequent sessions, or, at the very least, if the going gets rough in later sessions, you can remind the couple that mutual affection must be there, because you saw it.

Second, the technique helps the couple normalize their conflict. When they learn that what is happening to them tends to happen to most couples, they can relax a little about the severity of their pathology, at least for a while. Now, they may have a glimmer of hope in what felt like a hopeless situation.

Practice Example

Julie sought counseling because her husband was "addicted to the Internet." Julie and David had been married 9 years and had two children under age 5. David worked as the manager of the produce department of a grocery store, and Julie was a stay-at-home mom.

Their problems started 2 years ago, when David began spending more and more time on the Internet. Initially, Julie joined him in a game that involved teams, and she enjoyed their time together playing and planning strategies. However, after a while, she became bored with it and tired of spending so much time in the same activity. Although her interest waned, his did not. On the contrary, his time spent on the computer increased steadily. Her protests fell on deaf ears as his obsession with the computer increased. Now, he frequented chat rooms in addition to continuing to play the game.

They became more and more distant. The frequency of sexual encounters decreased until several months would go by with no sexual activity at all. Julie did not think he was visiting porn sites to get his needs met, but she was not sure. She partially blamed herself for his lack of interest because she had gained weight since the birth of her last child.

By the time she made an appointment with me, she was at the end of her rope. David's lack of interest in her and the children was beyond distressing; it was unacceptable. She was contemplating filing for divorce but decided to see a therapist first and explore her options.

At my suggestion, she asked David to attend marital therapy with her. When he refused, they had a big fight and she told him to get out, that it was over. After spending one night out of the house, he relented and complied with her request for therapy.

After obtaining both Julie's and David's perception of why they were in therapy, I asked them to give me an account of how their relationship began and what attracted each to the other in the first place.

I learned that they met at a church function when she was 13 and he was 17. Her family allowed her to be in the company of this older boy because he was the preacher's kid and was therefore "safe." They laughed together remembering that misconception! From that point, they were together on-and-off, with both experiencing other relationships periodically until they finally married.

She volunteered that he was typically the one who broke up with her to date others. When I asked if her perception was that she was historically more invested in the relationship than he was, she replied, "Absolutely!" Finally, while they were engaged, she met someone else. She gave the ring back and pursued the other guy. David was undone by this uncharacteristic move on her part, and he really worked to get her back. Finally, he won her over, and they were married.

Their list of attractions and the condition of those attractions now follows. David said:

1. He was attracted by her obvious maturity at such a young age. Now, she acts like his mother, always griping and scolding him for being on the computer.

2. She shared his interest; they had a lot in common. Now, she is not interested in anything he likes to do. In fact, she is not interested in him.

3. The two of them would talk for hours; they communicated well, and she was a good listener. Now, they don't even talk.

4. He was physically attracted to her. Now, his lack of interest is known to both of them.

5. He liked her strength. She was sure of herself, confident. Now, that strength and self-confidence might be used to leave him.

Julie said:

1. She was physically attracted to him. Now, she still is. That has not changed.

2. They had a lot in common. He liked the same things that she did, and they enjoyed just being together. Now, all he wants to do is spend time on the computer. Sometimes, it feels like they have nothing in common anymore.

3. He was older, wiser, someone she could lean on. Now, he acts like a little boy, always playing games and not tending to the responsibilities of a husband and father.

4. They could communicate well. He listened to her, and they could talk about anything. Now, it was all surface. They seldom had conversations with any depth anymore.

When we completed the three components of this technique—the story of their meeting, what attracted them, and the status of that attraction today—we had about 10 minutes left in the session. I used that time to make a preliminary diagnosis, define my requirements for therapy, and assign a plan of action.

A Therapeutic Direction

The success of the technique in the case of this couple was in relating the history of their relationship to me. When I heard that they were only 13 and 17 when they met, I thought, "Uh-oh! This may not work!" I was afraid they wouldn't even remember their attractions at that early age, and I feared that their immaturity might impede the meaningfulness of that initial meeting. I was both right and wrong. Although they did recall those initial attractions, the more compelling memory was of her giving the ring back when they were engaged. As she recounted that story, they both softened visibly. For the first time, he looked at her with real affection, and she responded to that look with a flirtatious twinkle. Clearly, like now, when the tables are turned and he risks losing her, he rallies to save the relationship. That was the clue I needed to know where to go with them.

I told them that my preliminary diagnosis was that it appeared there was a lot of hope for this marriage. There were some difficult problems, but there was also a level of commitment and affection between them. I told them that if they decided to work with me, they had to commit to three requirements:

1. Attend a therapy session once a week for 8 weeks.

2. Have at least one date per week. The date is to be arranged by David, and Julie is to arrange child care. The date is only for the two of them—no kids, no friends, and no family.

3. Refrain from sex until further notice.

Rules 1 and 2 are the usual ones I use for marital therapy, and I use Rule 3 if there are problems in the sexual arena (see Chapter 14, "Resurrecting the Dead Relationship").

The couple agreed to the stipulations, and, after scheduling an appointment for the next week, left the office smiling at one another. Certainly, the future for this couple was uncertain, but this technique had at least provided an opportunity for healing and reconciliation.

The Paper Exercise

This tool is one of my favorites; the more I use it, the sharper it becomes. The couples I see are usually motivated to seek therapy for one of several reasons: (a) They are seeking greater intimacy through improved communication, (b) they need help dealing with conflict, or (c) they are in crisis. The Paper Exercise is an excellent diagnostic tool that is informative and effective in all of these scenarios. It is adapted from *The Couples Journey* by Susan Campbell, PhD.

Sometimes, couples seeking therapy will say that their goal for therapy is to "make our relationship better" or "increase the intimacy between us." It may not be so easy for the therapist to get a grip on the issues. Is there a covert power struggle? If there is, how is it played out? What are the weapons? Is enmeshment a factor? What about temperament, lifestyle, and value differences? What about dreams for the future? The Paper Exercise may illuminate the area of concern and provide a direction for therapy.

Couples often complain of problems in "communication," but they have a hard time articulating just what they mean and can't come up with good examples themselves. This tool allows the therapist to sample a piece of the couple's communication right on the spot.

If a crisis (e.g., infidelity, major conflict, imminent separation) propels a couple into therapy, the therapist has a pressing agenda and would, of course, go with that initially. However, below the surface of the presenting crisis are deep waters, supporting an ecosystem all their own. This tool allows the clinician to do some below-the-surface exploration with couples after the storm dies down.

NOTE: The paper exercise is adapted from Susan Campbell, *The Couples Journey,* San Luis Obispo, CA: Impact. Copyright © 1980 by Susan Campbell. Used by permission.

Instructions

Tell your couple that you have an exercise you would like them to do. Show them a piece of paper (I use a clean piece of copy paper). Say that the paper is symbolic. Looking directly at one partner, explain that the paper represents something very important to him or her, something highly valued and dear. Then, looking at the other partner, say that the paper represents exactly the same to him or her; something very important, highly valued, and dear. Now, ask them to hold the paper and tell them that their task is this: At the end of 10 minutes, only one of them may hold the paper. They cannot cut or tear or divide the paper in any way, but they may do all the talking they want. Only one person ends up holding the paper; they have up to 10 minutes.

I am careful not to use the word "decision" or "decide." Actually, that is the point—you are asking the couple to come to a decision together, and you will be observing their decision-making process carefully, looking for information about skills (or lack thereof) in negotiating, sharing, listening, respectfulness, and attentiveness, to name a few. The exercise might not be as genuine or as close to their usual communication pattern if the therapist defines the objective (make a decision) for them.

Some couples will want to quiz you about the instructions. I usually just repeat what I said before, and avoid specifics. For example, if I'm asked, "Now, just what does the paper stand for?" I'll say what I said in the first place, that it represents something very important, highly valued, and dear to each of them. If one of them asks, "Can we talk?" I'll tell them that they may do all the talking they want. Couples are often nervous and hesitant to start, so I usually look at my watch and say, "Go," to help them along. Most couples complete the exercise well within the time allotted, although I've had a few who could not get the job done in 10 minutes.

Diagnostic Suggestions

You will be amazed at how much information you will glean in such a short time using this tool. On numerous occasions, I have seen the couple complete the exercise in less than 10 seconds. In those instances, one of two things happens: Either one partner will snatch the paper from the other, or one partner will let go of the paper almost immediately. Sometimes, the other person sits there with a look of total surprise on his or her face; sometimes, the look is all too knowing. You have lots to talk about! Ask the partner who either snatched the paper or let it go (thus making a unilateral decision of who holds the paper) questions such as the following:

- Why did you do that?
    - He or she may not be sure why. You can explore further: Could it be impulsivity? How does that play itself out in the relationship?
    - Is it about fear? Of what? Why?
    - Is it about powerlessness? If other tactics have failed through the years, a quick response may be the only way to gain, or keep, some degree of power in the relationship.
    - Is the snatcher/releaser controlling and domineering in the relationship?
    - Was the other's acceptance of the unilateral decision (snatching or releasing) assumed? Why or why not?
- Is it usual that you are the one who makes the decisions?
- Were you/are you comfortable with what you did?
    - Sometimes, the identified decision maker is not so comfortable with the job. He or she may want more input from the other but does not know how to ask for it.
    - The reaction may be in response to an attempt to meet the other's expectations.
    - Some individuals with a high need for control are very fear-based. The unspoken concern may be, "If I'm not in control, who is?" You might also want to ask: Was there a time when someone else was in control and bad things happened to you?
- How do you think your partner feels about your reaction?

The following questions can be asked of the partner left empty-handed or left "holding the bag":

- Were you surprised?
- How did that make you feel?
    - This rather trite and overused idiom is perfect in this instance because you have created an opportunity for an honest and safe response (assuming domestic abuse is not part of the problem). I have heard statements like, "I feel like I don't count, that my opinion doesn't matter" or "She's left me with all the responsibility, and I don't like it!" or "He never really listens to my side of the story anyway. How does that make me feel? Stupid."
- What could have happened that would have been better for you?

After helping them explore the experience, I suggest that it would be helpful to do some work on communication. The Paper Exercise revealed that they were apt to make decisions with very little information shared between them. For example, what were they making a decision about in the exercise? Neither partner asked what the paper represented to the other, so did they really know what was at stake?

This is a real eye-opener to many couples. Suddenly, they are able to see that at least some of their problems have to do with the way they communicate (or don't communicate). Sometimes, one or both partners say that they didn't ask what the paper represented because they already knew what the paper meant to the other. Be sure to check that out. They are often incorrect!

Not all couples snatch or relinquish the paper. But it is not uncommon that the couple may talk about everything but what the paper represents. I have seen couples use up all their time considering options about who will end up holding the paper without ever revealing to one another what it means. If that is the case, you have a pretty good clue that they need assistance discovering the meaning behind their behavior with each other across the board.

Be prepared for conflict! Some power struggles are overt. Issues with trust surface as well. One partner may not relinquish the paper to the other because he or she does not trust the other with it, and that is often verbalized. This is very helpful to your treatment planning if trust issues have not come up in previous sessions. Now you have another direction in which to go.

Value differences may emerge if the couple does discuss what the paper represents. I remember a husband's anguished expression when his wife told him the paper represented God. "Of course it's God!" he lamented. "That's the problem, you give God a hell of a lot more attention than you give me!"

A more common variation on a values theme is when one spouse puts the children first and the other does not, or when both say the paper represents the children. I agree with John and Linda Friel, authors of *The 7 Worst Things (Good) Parents Do,* when they say that one of the worst things parents can do is to put their relationship with the children before their relationship with each other. (See the "Suggested Reading" section at the end of this chapter for details.)

Practice Example

William and Rosita had been in therapy for 2 months. They had been married for 11 years and did not have children. William, a banker, was reserved and quiet, and Rosita, an elementary school teacher, was fiery and outspoken. The issue that brought them to therapy was conflict over the thermostat.

Rosita explained that she was usually cold and liked the house to be plenty warm in the winter. William was never cold. "And even if I were, that's what sweaters are for. If the house is a little chilly, put on a sweater!" he said with exasperation.

For most of the first session, they behaved like a couple of opposing attorneys, vying for the judge's favor. I could see that I was cast as the magistrate. No stone was left unturned as each one defended his or her position, and cross-examination of the other's position was grueling. It was tense in the courtroom!

The agenda that the couple brought to the first session was metaphorical for a prevailing dynamic. Rosita saw her husband as parsimonious in every arena. In an individual session with me, she gave examples: He wanted her to use the toilet after him each morning so they would have to flush only once. On long trips, he drove well below the speed limit in order to save money. They had had no real vacation in 5 years. He even chiseled his way out of buying her a wedding ring; they used her mother's ring. He promised her one of her own when they got their feet on the ground. Well, now they were doing quite well, but a new ring had never appeared. She was sick of what she called his hoarding and withholding behavior. Finally, she said, "He likes his showers lukewarm and drippy; I like mine hot and powerful. That about says it all!" She wanted out!

William's psychological testing revealed that he had a need to present himself as strong and adequate. Clinical scales yielded evidence of tremendous stability. Test results also indicated that he appeared remote and had a tendency to intellectualize away all feelings. In individual sessions, he acknowledged that saving the marriage seemed hopeless given Rosita's long history of anger and dissatisfaction with him. He saw Rosita as beautiful and exciting. He loved her energy and enthusiasm for life; however, she had a tendency to be irresponsible. She was a woman of excess, and if he did not keep the lid on her tendency for extravagance, they would not have anything. He was distressed that maybe he was turning out to be like his stingy, tightwad father after all—something he had fought against all his life.

These conflicted partners could identify the positive characteristics that attracted them to each other initially. (See Chapter 11, "The Couple's Love Story.") Genuine affection was apparent as they recalled these qualities. Rosita was attracted to William's stability. She liked his genuine, honest approach to life; he had no "hidden agendas," she said. William saw Rosita as a "beautiful lady," with excellent social skills. She was fun to be with and interesting.

On the sixth session, I introduced the Paper Exercise. The task energized Rosita. She sat on the edge of the sofa, her eyes sparkling. William was characteristically contained and unemotional. He sat back with his legs crossed. When I said, "Go," Rosita playfully snatched the paper away from William. Before I could say anything, she said, "Just teasing!" and offered the paper back to him.

This couple talked about what the paper symbolized to them and agreed on its meaning. A close relationship with God and the importance of family were the values identified.

"I think I should hold the paper," Rosita began.

William laughed in response and said, "Of course you do! That's the whole problem! You want to do things your way; if I have another perspective, you accuse me of being a stick-in-the-mud or a party-pooper or a chauvinist!"

"But you never, and I mean never, take my ideas seriously! It's as if anything I say is wrong or irrational or stupid!"

"I've never said you were stupid, and I don't think you are."

"Oh, come on, William! You didn't even like what I picked out for your sister's baby shower last week! A baby shower! That's a woman thing, and you still criticized my choice! I can't do anything to suit you!"

"You have a point, Rosie," he responded, looking sad. "I'm sure I go overboard sometimes; well, I know I do. And I'm willing to work on it."

"I don't want all that much; just a little respect and the opportunity to be right now and then," she said softly, looking intently into his eyes.

"I'm willing to change some, but I'm not willing to change my whole self; sometimes, I think you want me to be an entirely different person. I am who I am, Rosie."

"I don't want you to change who you are, just loosen up on some stuff a little."

"I can try."

"You get credit for trying."

Within the 10 minutes, Rosita relinquished the paper to her husband. Now I could see that her iron-clad resolve to leave the marriage had soft edges, and William saw it, too. She overstated her position of belief that the marriage was over like she overstated many things. Her confidence in William's strength and stability was evidenced when she let him "hold" the things most dear to her.

William and Rosita were in therapy for a relative short period of time, only a few more weeks. William was intentional about loosening his grip on many issues, and Rosita came to see that his practical, methodical personality was an anchor that allowed her to bounce and bob around on the surface of life in her free-spirited way, but kept her from drifting into dangerous water.

Suggested Reading

Campbell, S. (1980). *The couple's journey.* San Luis Obispo, CA: Impact. Available
   from the author at www.SusanCampbell.com
Friel, J. C., & Friel, L. D. (1999). *The 7 worst things (good) parents do.* Deerfield
   Beach, FL: Health Communications.

Between a Rock and a Hard Place
Letting Go

The older I get, the more I believe that life is all about letting go. It appears to me that the more a person can relax that frantic grasp on life, the better. The prevailing fantasy is that there is a way to ensure personal and emotional security; I don't think so. The clients I have seen clutching onto people and situations in a valiant but vain attempt to control things are legion. They are also unhappy. How can we as therapists help our clients loosen their grip and try a different approach? This tool is one way. (It also works well in individual therapy.)

Instructions

Near the end of a session, present your couple with a selection of rocks. I keep mine in an antique wire basket that is in my office as part of the decor. You might want to use a lovely wooden box for your rocks, or a decorative tin or canister. Ask each partner to choose a rock to keep. I usually discuss the nature of a rock: It's hard; it holds its shape no matter what; it can be used as a weapon; and it can be something you need (if you are building a wall) or something that you need to remove (if you are preparing the soil for a garden). Then, ask this question: What is the hard place in you that needs to soften?

Instruct each person to take his or her rock home and put it someplace where it will be seen often, as a reminder of the hard place inside that needs to soften. Ask both partners to write an answer to the question and bring it to the next session. Challenge them to offer specific solutions, that is, how would each one behave that would be soft compared to their behavior now?

Materials

You'll need a selection of rocks, from which your clients can make their choice. I use those pretty, smooth, shiny river rocks that you can find in the garden section of discount stores or in nurseries. They aren't expensive, and they just look special. You may have a rock shop in your area. If so, that would be a great place to find your "therapy rocks."

Practice Example for Couples Therapy

Michelle and Paul had been married for 12 years. They had one child, a boy age 8. They sought marital therapy because of the distance between them and the atmosphere of resentment.

The lack of warmth or positive regard between this couple was right on the surface. Although they were polite and respectful enough in conversation, it was a teeth-gritting, controlled pleasantness.

There were a number of surface issues. Their communication style was ineffective, and they had control issues, in-law problems, and a conflict over finances. We dabbled around with first one and then another of these concerns for several weeks. I felt we were slapping on paint and washing windows when, in reality, the foundation was seriously cracked. Over time, they led me to the basement, and we looked at the structural damage.

Part of Paul's initial attraction to Michelle was that she was her own person. When they met, she was an attorney in a large law firm, and he was a CPA. They were representing the same client, a family-owned business, in a lawsuit. Paul was attracted to the pretty young lawyer and impressed by her knowledge and self-confidence. They moved in together after 8 months of dating and got married the next year.

Things were great for the next 4 years. When Michelle became pregnant, they talked about a maternity leave. She would stay home with the baby for the first year; that was 8 years ago. Michelle never went back to work, and although it was unspoken between them, Paul resented it very much. His independent, corporate-savvy wife had turned into a housewife who drove carpool and worried over wallpaper patterns. She defended her stay-home status as a mother's right and pulled out all the stops to make Paul feel guilty if he so much as mentioned the possibility that she enter the workforce again.

The other huge crack in the foundation was the affair that Paul had 5 years ago. He was on an out-of-town assignment when he met a woman who worked in the hospital that his company was auditing. She was an administrator at the hospital, and she had all of the attributes that once attracted him to his wife. She was attractive, independent, smart, and aggressive. She was equally smitten by the ruddy, auburn-haired CPA and open to a relationship with him. They kept the affair going until Michelle confronted him with records from his cell phone bill.

The pattern was cast for their ongoing volley: She used the affair to punish him, and he used his position as the sole breadwinner to control her. Until this match stopped, they would never be able to play doubles.

After a thorough exploration of this dynamic, I suggested the Between a Rock and a Hard Place exercise. Two weeks later, they brought their writing assignments to session with them.

Michelle wrote about the affair as the most traumatic event of her life. The idea that Paul could find comfort in the arms of another woman devastated her. It also humiliated her. How could she have let things between them get that bad? What did another woman have that she did not have? On one level, she was the injured party and deserved to be upset for a long time. On another level, she knew she used the affair to manipulate Paul. It would be risky to let go of this weapon. She would be defenseless, an easy target. However, she truly loved Paul and wanted the marriage to work. Therefore, she would let go of, in her words, "Throwing the rock of the affair at you every time we have an argument."

Paul's promise was to let go of his anger that Michelle wanted to stay home; she did not really have to work anyway. He made an adequate income, and although their lifestyle would be different if she also brought in a salary, her role as mother to their son was extremely important. He would let go of his mind-set of how things should be, and learn to accept and enjoy things as they were.

Although therapy was not over by a long shot, it was the first sign that each of them was willing to change in order to make their marriage work; at that point in therapy, it counted for a lot.

Practice Example for Individual Therapy

Lois came to therapy because of "family problems" and anxiety. She had been troubled with anxiety in the past and stated, "Historically, I pull in and withdraw from people. I don't want to do that this time, I want to handle things differently."

The anxiety had been triggered by having to place her ill, elderly mother in a nursing home. Her mother and father were divorced and had not remarried, so Lois and her brother were the next of kin for both of their parents. Her mother did not want to go to a nursing home and was angry about her daughter's involvement in the decision to place her in one. Lois said, "First, Mother cut me off (emotionally and financially), then she died a few months later."

Her father, age 92 and in poor health as well, still lived independently in his home. Lois explained that she had a brother who was "irresponsible" and "slow"; the brother lived down the street from their father in a small rural community. Her father was known to make large financial gifts to her brother periodically, but not to her, because "Joe needed help, and I guess I didn't."

There were other issues as well. Lois had lost an adult daughter to cancer just 1 year ago. Although her daughter's husband and the children lived out of state, Lois had been very involved in settling her daughter's financial affairs. Her daughter named her as a beneficiary on her life insurance policy, but all the funds were used to pay outstanding bills (mostly medical). Lois enjoyed a close relationship with her surviving daughter, who lived with her family in another state.

Lois divorced the father of her daughters after 24 years of marriage, and she had not remarried. She was a retired schoolteacher and now worked at a gift shop part-time.

It was difficult to get a grasp on Lois's core issue. She would flit from one story to another in session, and it was tough to find a common theme. Over time, one emerged—it was financial. Lois was always the bridesmaid and never the bride. Her husband had not earned a substantial income during their life together and was not much help with the children after the divorce. It seemed that taking responsibility for herself by obtaining secure employment was punished rather than rewarded. Her parents were apt to buy a car for her errant brother or give him large sums of money periodically because he had a hard time of it financially. She, on the other hand, received nothing.

When her daughter died, it was tragic enough. But watching the sizable amount of funds from the life insurance policy slip through her fingers was dismal as well. It finally became clear to me that she held out hope that she would become a woman of means when her (quite wealthy) father died. In fact, she had been clinging to the fantasy of wealth for many years. It always seemed to be right around the corner.

During her course of therapy with me, the fantasy was threatened again when her father chose to move to a nursing home close to her brother instead of one near her. Did this mean that she would, at best, inherit substantially less than her brother, or, at worst, be cut off once again from inheriting? Her angst was the result of a dream of wealth that had solidified inside her like a rock.

We talked about how the fantasy of wealth had affected her life. As long as the hope/dream/desire/promise of money loomed in her consciousness, her life was on hold in many ways. I introduced the rock technique, suggesting that if she could soften the hardened place inside her (the hope of wealth), she might be free indeed. Free to possibilities she had not considered. Free to be truly independent. Free of her father's control. Free in her spirit.

The rock metaphor was just what I needed to help her conceptualize the system that was driving her anxiety. She chose a rock to represent the hardness inside her, the dream of inheritance—something she wanted to let go of. We worked on this theme for several more sessions, focusing on her desire not to withdraw and isolate, as was her pattern in the past. She became more active in her synagogue, and she joined a group that met during the week to read and discuss various spiritual topics. She began exercising with a seniors' aerobic class at the community center. She devoted more time to her garden. Our work in therapy changed; we focused more on the reality of her daily life as it was instead of worrying about what it might be or could be. We talked a lot about being present in the moment (see Chapter 8, "Every Now and Zen").

Lois blossomed. She even looked different; she smiled more often and became more attractive. We were in the process of terminating therapy when her father died. She did claim a nice inheritance after all; you never know what letting go will mean.

Resurrecting the
Dead Relationship

In couples work, the "patient" is the relationship, that invisible entity that occupies the empty space between partners who sit in the therapist's office. The sad thing is that the patient doesn't always make it to the hospital soon enough. All too often, the relationship is gasping its last breath when the therapist finally has the opportunity to examine it.

Because of many couples' reluctance to seek help until it's too late, therapists get a bad rap. Our services are suspect because many of our patients die; it's a vicious circle.

But the ones we do save are worth it. Restoring a relationship to health and happiness is rewarding work indeed! This is not to say that putting a dead relationship to rest is not important or rewarding work. I think some of the best work we do is helping people recognize and accept that there has been a death. Preparing the body for burial and supporting the survivors as it is laid to rest is a crucial service to render. But this tool is for those relationships that still have the possibility of recovery.

One of the common relational pathologies that leads to a slow and prolonged death could be called "drift disorder." Chief complaints include statements such as, "We've grown apart over the years; we just don't seem to have much in common anymore" or "We never have fun anymore; our life together is so lackluster!" You might hear, "There's more to life than this; I'm not willing to accept what this relationship has become." One partner might say, "I'm bored to death with him! If something doesn't change, I'm out of here!" or "I'm not sure what the matter is, but I don't feel romantic toward her like I used to."

When presented with symptoms like these, I always look for the interest quotient when I have each partner in an individual session. If there is absolutely no physical or sexual interest or attraction to the other, the condition may be terminal. I have never had a client (or a friend) who could get that back once it is gone. When clients come to therapy wanting to know if I can help them recover the romantic feelings they once had for their partner, I ask them if they would be interested in touching, smelling, or caressing their partner again. Then, I watch carefully for the body language that accompanies the answer. If the answer is no, accompanied by a shudder or a slight recoil into the chair, in my book, it's already a dead issue. As you might suspect, the number of women with the shudder/recoil response is much higher than the number of men.

This tool is for those couples that have a positive or even neutral response to the issue of interest and attraction.

Instructions

I always begin this process with the tool found in Chapter 11, "The Couple's Love Story." This enables them to remember and articulate all of the attraction that brought them together in the first place. Then, I talk about how crucial it will be for them to change, and how difficult change is. The trouble is, the pattern into which they've drifted has been functional for some time, even if it is bad. They are still together. Therefore, the pattern is powerful.

The pattern is finite, however, or they would not be in a therapist's office. No one is happy, and someone has said that this can't go on forever. In other words, the drifting nature of the current in which they are caught will eventually dash them against the rocks. The task, then, is to repair the engine and determine the course the vessel will take. To get the process started, the sleepy crew must be alerted. At this moment, the couple has experienced a wake-up call.

To facilitate a change of course, I suggest separating the couple. This takes on a variety of forms. Sometimes, it means one partner moves to the lake house or establishes a separate residence. I have had clients who rented an apartment month to month. Some clients were house-sitters for friends who were traveling, and others have moved in with family or friends for a while.

Not all couples can arrange a way to live in separate residences for a while. In those cases, it means one partner moves out of the bedroom and down the hall to a different one. If that is not possible, there's always the sofa! It might mean the couple stops contacting each other (phoning, e-mailing, meeting for lunch, etc.) during the day. Somehow, some way, a distinct change of course must be established. An intentional separation is the first step.

Once a separation, albeit artificial, is accomplished, you can start over (so to speak). Couples may need a lot of therapy support at this time. It is usually a scary proposition to at least one of the partners, if not both. Although the couple may be complaining about their unhappiness together, divorce may be their greatest fear. "Separation" can translate as the first scoot down that slippery slide. Therefore, I like to see the partners in individual sessions during the first few weeks of the separation. By seeing them individually, you can render support and tease out individual issues. Try to get your couple to agree to at least 2 weeks of separation before beginning the couples work. You might not get that much time, because some couples are just too threatened; that's OK, but don't give up without a fuss.

After the 2-week waiting period, introduce the weekly date. Designate one partner as the one responsible for asking and arranging the date; the other is responsible for arranging child care (if necessary). In a sense, this starts the relationship over; it's a "first date." Now you have the opportunity to assess the courting behavior of each. Social skills, including flirting and dating etiquette, are learned behaviors. You may be surprised at how little your couple knows! You can step in as teacher or coach with suggestions and information that is very useful. Be sure to ask for a report on the date in each session.

The physical separation includes sexual separation as well. I instruct my couple firmly that there is to be *no* sexual contact between them until I say so. This tactic may seem autocratic to some therapists, but it is an unbeatable power tool. First, it diffuses the pressure for sex that one of the partners inevitably feels. Although this is not an ironclad rule, it seems that one partner is always less interested in maintaining the relationship than the other. It's a rule of thumb in divorce mediation work that one of the partners is further down the path to dissolution than the other, and it seems to apply in couples work as well. In my experience, many women become conditioned against sensuality with their mate. For years, every time he touched her affectionately, she ended up flat on her back. No wonder she doesn't crave his touch, and even jumps when he tries to kiss her neck when she's standing at the kitchen sink! This rule allows her to quit worrying about where things will go. They won't go anywhere.

Second, there is nothing sweeter than forbidden fruit. When I make this proclamation, couples often laugh hysterically, as if not having sexual contact would be a problem. They haven't had sex for . . . months! Let them laugh. You have just changed the dynamic. Now, they are not *allowed* to have sex.

This is nothing new. I am borrowing from the principles of sensate therapy, which has been around therapeutic circles for years; it's the frontline approach for sexual dysfunction. But not everyone studies sexual dysfunction in graduate school, and one could miss seminars or workshops that cover the concept. This tool is fashioned from the basics of sensate therapy, which is great stuff even if sexual dysfunction is not the presenting issue.

If you have facilitated a 2-week separation, and have seen both partners in individual therapy, it is time to begin the couples work in earnest. Tools in this book may be helpful in that there is often not much of an agenda with these couples. There may not be any insurmountable conflict to manage or compelling issues to explore. The Paper Exercise (Chapter 12), the Talking Stick (Chapter 16), and A Soulful Relationship (Chapter 17) may be helpful in generating material.

Next, I suggest that the couple plan an evening or two at home, along with their date night. If there are children in the home, this step should wait until the children have gone to bed (so that the couple has privacy). There is nothing like a foot massage to establish intimate contact in a safe and nonthreatening way. Invite your couple to explore the delights of sitting on the sofa together feet to feet. In that position, the partners are looking directly at one another, and each has access to the other's feet. This won't work if the people are too big for the sofa, of course, and modifications are fine, but use this position if you can. Shoes and socks should be removed so that the touch is skin to skin. Each partner gets a foot rub from the other, one at a time. Emphasize that rubbing each other's feet at the same time is not the way to go. Each should have the opportunity to only receive. If you are giving at the same time you are receiving, it just isn't the same. (Note: I use this technique when working with couples on sexuality. Often, one partner insists on mutual orgasm, and the other isn't coming through. Using the foot massage as an example, it becomes apparent really fast that taking turns is not such a bad deal!) I suggest that they make the setting as romantic as possible. Turn off the lights, use a candle or two, play soft music, have a glass of wine together, and so on. Remind them that the no-sexual-contact rule still applies. The foot rub goes no further.

The timing for these steps will vary from couple to couple. That is, you may have one couple who practice the foot rub for 3 weeks before moving to the next step, and another who practice the foot rub only 1 week before moving on. For example, if your couple get only eight visits on their managed care plan, you don't have the luxury of walking through each step with them and assigning lengthy practice times as I am describing here. If that is the case, accommodate your couple as best you can. You might prepare a handout that outlines what step to take when.

After the foot rub has been integrated into the life of the couple, move to the next step. This week, they need to arrange a time when they can be alone together in the bedroom. Clothing is removed except for underwear. This step is a tactile experience, an exploration of touch. Each partner has a turn touching and receiving touch. Again, no sexual touch is allowed. Tell them to collect a variety of objects to produce different tactile sensations. A feather is excellent, as are netting and sponges. Small kitchen items like mushroom brushes or toothpicks are good choices; cool and warm objects are also good. Tell them to be creative. Anything goes.

The partner receiving the touch lies on the bed, face down, and the other lightly moves first one, then another, object over his or her exposed skin. It is important to create a pleasing, relaxing atmosphere as well. Candles and music enhance the experience. The object is to help the couple discover (or rediscover) their sensuality. The no-sexual-contact rule is still in force, so they are free to really participate in the sensations created without fear or pressure of what comes next.

After a week, or two or three, of practicing, introduce the next step. It is the same scenario, only this time, massage is used as the tactile stimulant instead of the objects. Again, underwear is on, and no sexual activity is allowed. Encourage the couple to return to any or all of the preliminary steps at will.

Next, the underwear goes, and sexual touch is allowed, but no intercourse. Few couples tend to make it this far. Usually, when I ask about their progress in session, they sit and giggle at one another like a couple of teenagers caught making out in the backseat of a car. Sometimes, they disappear from therapy about this time, and I chalk it off as success.

To summarize, here are the steps involved in resurrecting a relationship:

1. A strategic separation

2. A date night and the no-sex rule

3. Foot rub

4. Tactile experience with objects (no sex)

5. Body massage (underwear on, no sex)

6. Body massage (underwear off, sexual touch only, no intercourse)

7. If your couple somehow made it through Step 6 and are just waiting for your OK, now's the time to give it to them!

If intercourse has not occurred by now, find out why not. It is not physiologically normal for a middle-aged man to have episodic impotence; if this is the case, refer your client to a medical doctor.

If intercourse has occurred, find out if it was satisfying for both parties. A high percentage of women do not achieve orgasm through intercourse. If your woman is inorgasmic, you have two ways to go. You can teach her about self-gratification (masturbation), so she can, in turn, teach her partner how to satisfy her, or you can refer her to someone who is comfortable and skilled in working with sexual issues.

Practice Example

A former client referred her friend and colleague to me. Sarah was a paralegal in a large firm of attorneys. She was clearly nervous; she fidgeted around on my sofa, crossing and uncrossing her legs and shifting her weight around to change positions. It was about her husband, she said. Gary was a dentist. They had been married for 6 years and had no children. Everything seemed just fine until she realized that it wasn't. He wasn't interested in her like he used to be. He spent the majority of his evenings at home in his office on the computer. He never seemed to want her company. They joined a fitness center several years ago, but now he did not seem to care whether she went with him to exercise. He was no longer eager to share his day with her at dinner, and even his eye contact across the table was not good. He begged off going with her to her sister's in Oklahoma over the Fourth of July as they had always done; she went alone. When she tried to elicit his input on the wallpaper she was choosing for the bedroom, he told her to pick whatever she wanted, it did not really matter to him.

She had tried everything she knew to do. She fixed his favorite meals and baked his favorite desserts. She bought new lingerie and changed the style of her hair. Nothing worked. She was afraid he was having an affair. So was I! All the symptoms were there. What else could it be?

Gary knew she had an appointment with a therapist. She told him she was very unhappy and had been for some time. He was supportive of her decision and agreed to be involved if it was advised. I suggested that the next session should be an individual session with Gary; Sarah was comfortable with that.

I see this pattern all too often. One of the partners in a relationship wants out and doesn't know how to do it. Guiding a partner to the exit door is not an uncommon task for a therapist, and I thought I had this one figured out before I ever saw Gary. When I did, things did not go as anticipated. I'm pretty good at getting the truth out of the wandering partner, especially if he or she can see that I am not judging his or her behavior. But with Gary, I could not get to first base with my theory. He denied not only having an affair, but also having any interest in another woman. He wasn't lying.

He knew that his wife was unhappy and felt terrible about it, but he could not escape the reality of feeling apathetic about their marriage lately. He was sick and tired of her obsession with him. Everything in her life revolved around him. He wished she would get a life! Her only other interest was her family, and he was certainly sick of them! He had refused to go to her sister's for the holiday because he could not tolerate one more family gathering. His family was distant and disconnected, all right, but hers was ridiculous! Wasn't there a happy medium?

Now I had something with which to work. Sarah and Gary began couples therapy the next week. Their reaction to the Couple's Love Story was hopeful. Both were visibly moved in their recounting of how they met and what drew them to the other. Following that session, I saw them again in individual sessions. When working with Sarah, I explored her life apart from Gary and her family. He was correct, there wasn't much there. She acknowledged that he had become so much the focus of her life that she had neglected nurturing relationships with other women. Although she had women friends at work and at church, she did little to expand those associations. The more distant Gary became, the closer to home she wanted to be.

Her family was another story. As much as she loved and needed them, she could see Gary's point. Most of her social energy was absorbed by those relationships; a better balance made sense. We also discussed the notion that Sarah's attraction and commitment to her family could be different from Gary's; maybe she could enjoy family gatherings without him on occasion, without the fear that there was something bad or abnormal about that.

Gary jumped on the idea of a separation, and Sarah was scared to death. She became a little more comfortable with the notion when I assured her that it was standard policy. Gary wanted to move out, but they had just purchased a new house the year before and couldn't afford a second residence. We settled on the following: Sarah would use her vacation time to visit her sister in Kansas City. That would create a whole week of separation. They agreed not to call or make contact during that week. While she was gone, Gary would move into the guest bedroom.

By the time the next session rolled around, Sarah and Gary had been apart for more than a week, and he had moved to another bedroom. I instituted the plan, starting with a date night. As the plan unfolded, I worked mostly with Sarah individually. She joined an aerobics class at the fitness center and started attending her church again (without Gary). She spent time with her family on her own and arranged to have lunch with women friends she had not seen for some time. With support in therapy, she was able to loosen the reins on fretting about Gary—where he was, what he was doing, how he was feeling every minute. We also addressed her fear of divorce. She was able to see that she did not really want to be in a relationship where she was not loved and desired.

This couple wanted to stick with the date night arrangement for a few weeks before scheduling another session. After several weeks, Gary called and asked me what was next. We scheduled an appointment, and I gave the foot rub instructions. Two weeks later, they were ready for the next step.

After practicing the tactile and touch routine with their chosen objects, they scheduled another appointment, and I assigned the massage. We met the week after that, and I told them to continue with the massage, only this time, clothes were off and sexual touch was permitted, but no intercourse. A few days after that session, Gary appeared at my office, unscheduled, with an anxious look on his face. "What's next?" he queried eagerly. In other cases, this would be an inappropriate and unacceptable intrusion into the therapist's office, but this was funny! I gave him the go-ahead and told him to call me when they felt ready for another appointment. I never heard from them again. Case closed!

Jake Got a Dog

This technique uses the time-honored parable to make a therapeutic point. It could almost be considered a nail, tack, or hook, but it is so effective that I think it deserves a place in the main compartment of your toolbox.

The nice and polite way to introduce this great little metaphor would be to say that it is helpful when working with very independent or self-contained people who are struggling in a relationship. The not-so-nice way is to say that it gets through to narcissistic types who just don't get it. What they don't get is the concept of sharing, accommodating, giving, and putting the other's needs somewhere in their consciousness. I save this to use when other kinder, gentler suggestions fall on deaf ears. Everybody seems to finally understand when this tale is told.

Because an example from the therapist's personal life carries so much more weight than a made-up story, I confess that when I use this technique, I manipulate the truth. I say that Jake is my friend's son. Jake could be my nephew or cousin or neighbor, but I have settled on saying that Jake is my friend's son. Say what you like. Here's the story:

> My friend's son Jake is a successful young man in his early 30s. He has a terrific career as a stockbroker. He drives a new car and has a house in the best part of town. He belongs to a country club, plays golf, and is well liked by his colleagues and friends. He is a member of his local church and attends services regularly. The trouble is, Jake is lonely. He's had a number of relationships with women but could never seem to find just the right one. At this point, he's really ready to find a life partner, someone with whom to share things on a daily basis. As full and successful as his life is, he has discovered that it is not enough.
>
> Since the woman of his dreams had not appeared yet, Jake decided to get a dog. He figured a lovable and loving dog would be just the thing to provide the companionship he longed for until the real thing came along.

After several weeks of researching breeds on the Internet, Jake decided on a chocolate Labrador. He soon found a breeder not far from where he lived and made an appointment to pick out his dog. The Lab puppy was perfect. He was a beautiful specimen, friendly and frisky and smart. The pup attracted admirers wherever they went. But there was a problem.

Jake was used to his morning routine. He rolled out of bed at 6 a.m., showered, shaved, and went to his favorite coffeehouse to read the paper and have a light breakfast; now, he had to walk the dog. His wonderful routine was derailed.

He met his running buddy at the YMCA at noon on Mondays, Wednesdays, and Fridays. Over time, they had developed the perfect route. It took them through pleasant neighborhoods, and the several hills and inclines were just enough to challenge the pair without exhausting them completely. Their route took exactly 45 minutes. They showered in the next 15 minutes and ate at the same little café every time. It took an hour and 30 minutes from start to finish. Now, Jake had to go home every day during his lunch hour to let the dog out. As much as he liked the dog, he resented this intrusion on his perfect routine.

He played golf in a foursome with colleagues every Thursday right after work. The country club was just down the street from the office, making the transition from work to play quick and easy. They would all go to dinner together after their game. Now, Jake had to go all the way home right after work every day to let the dog out and give him some exercise. If he didn't, the dog would mess in the laundry room and be a quivering mass of unspent energy. Also, when Jake skipped going home to tend to the dog, he would be tormented with guilt through the entire evening.

After a couple of weeks, Jake took the dog back to the breeder. It was just too much trouble! It could have been perfect if only the dog didn't need so much!

Jake was alone again.

You will want to alter the Jake story to fit the circumstances of your clients. Jake as an affluent young man in the Midwest works for my clients, but yours may relate better to a story that approximates their culture more closely. "Jake" may need to be "Carlos," for example, and he may play baseball instead of golf. His material successes may be that he finished high school, works first shift at the Ford plant, and just bought a car.

The only way a relationship with another person will work is if there is a spirit of mutuality between the couple. A partnership is a give-and-take arrangement. Almost everyone agrees that a relationship is doomed if one partner does all the giving and the other does all the taking. Surprisingly, many good and well-meaning people have to be taught what it means to share. One would hope that the "one must share" message gets transmitted long before adulthood, but it does not always happen that way. Sometimes, we therapists are the ones left to take up the slack in teaching lessons that should have been learned long ago; we hope that we have the right tools.

Practice Example

Eric had been divorced from his third wife for 4 months when he met Jessica. She was everything he ever wanted; never was he so sure that this was the woman for him. Jessica was equally smitten by Eric. She had been married twice herself, and she felt that she was finally mature enough to make a good choice where men were concerned. Eric was responsible, generous, and kind, as well as fun and romantic.

Eric and his second wife had been in marital therapy with me several years earlier, so when disillusionment punctured the perfect balloon of delight in this new relationship with Jessica, he suggested they visit his old counselor.

I remembered what it was like to work with Eric and his second wife. They did not enter therapy until their marriage was in its death throes, so I did not have much to work with except their desire *not* to be divorced again (both had been married before). The crux of the conflict revolved around Eric's proclivity to run the show.

He was a self-made businessman who had succeeded far beyond his level of education or sophistication. He was street-smart and savvy. He was also highly impulsive, taking huge financial risks. Somehow, he usually landed on his feet when he jumped into a new venture, but it was hard for his wife to watch the fall as he juggled four or five balls in the air.

In business, he was the boss; he had all the ideas and made all the decisions. He was good to his employees, who were grateful for his leadership and generosity; they loved him. It all worked perfectly. Unfortunately, it did not work so well at home.

I was not surprised that the same issues were rearing their ugly heads in this new relationship. Jessica was a woman of substance and unaccustomed to being relegated to the back seat. If she wasn't driving, she expected to be riding shotgun. Eric felt crowded in the front seat with anyone else. For all his moxie, Eric could not understand why he had so much trouble with women. It would be so easy if they just did things his way, like at work.

The situation precipitating therapy occurred when Jessica was moving in with him. By then, they knew that their styles and pace were at opposite ends of the continuum. He was quick and impulsive, she slow and methodical. He was an early bird; she was a night owl. He loved to travel; she was a homebody. They had managed these differences successfully until the move.

He could not understand why it was hard for her to leave the home she had lived in for 18 years. It didn't make sense to him! And he was fed up with her episodic melancholy about moving. Why be sad? After all, he was providing a much finer residence.

He wanted to hire packers and movers. She wanted to pack her things herself. Why? It doesn't make sense when you can hire it done! What is the matter with her?

On moving day, when she expected his help with the incidentals of the move, he went fishing. Well, he couldn't think of anything he would be needed for, so why not? At the end of the grueling day, she confronted him about feeling discounted and deserted. He blew sky-high and stormed out, saying that maybe she'd better turn the moving van around and head back home.

In an individual session following the fracas over the move, Eric spoke of his fear of not making it with Jessica. He felt she was "the one," and yet here they were in the midst of conflict. This relationship stuff was so much trouble, yet he did not want to be alone. He wanted a life partner, and he wanted it to be Jessica. It was time to tell him the story of Jake and his dog.

Eric finally got it. We went on to talk about the reality of his situation. If he wanted Jessica in his life, he would have to learn to consider her perspectives, needs, and desires. In fact, any woman to whom he would be attracted—independent, intelligent, articulate—would expect to have equal input into relational decisions. In order for Eric to have what he wanted, he would have to make some changes.

The Jake story gave me a springboard from which to jump into the difficult arena of confronting a client's narcissistic tendencies. It also served as a model that I could use to talk about the fine art of balancing need fulfillment (i.e., getting one's needs met while meeting the other's needs as well).

16

The Talking Stick

Several years ago, a colleague and I attended an excellent seminar on couples therapy. The presenters were interesting and dynamic, and they even offered two techniques I felt I could take home and plug right in. One technique was a model for couples communication, and it was especially effective for high-conflict couples. I couldn't wait to get home and try it out.

I had my chance the very next week. I had seen Sam and Lydia twice. They had been married for 12 years. Lydia was dark and fiery, a proud woman who held her own. Sam was several years older than Lydia. He wore blue jeans with cowboy boots and plaid shirts. He was a hard-working man who struggled to maintain the authority he felt was his duty as head of the family. Sam took on four children when he married Lydia, and they had two more of their own. The stress incurred by a couple parenting six children almost goes without saying.

Among other issues, Sam and Lydia had communication problems. They were entrenched in a communication style punctuated by interruptions, defensiveness, and a degree of hopelessness (i.e., when conflict arose, they both gave up and threw in the towel quickly).

At the session following the seminar, I carefully explained the new technique that we would try in the office and they would practice at home. Part of the way through the instructions, Lydia interrupted me and said, "Oh! You mean the Talking Stick! My heritage is Native American; my people have been using this for hundreds of years!" So much for the expensive seminar and fancy new ideas. . . .

Maybe there are no new ideas, only old ones that are repackaged for new consumers. I am grateful for those among us who discover discarded relics from other eras and have the vision to foresee their contemporary relevance. Archetypal concepts like this one are not subject to the erosion of time, but they can be lost.

I love this simple but profound technique, and I offer it here without reference to my own teachers because the technique is apparently in the public domain.

Instructions

I have found that the most effective way to introduce the Talking Stick is to do it right in the middle of a couple's argument. Of course, you wouldn't want to interrupt a conflict if there was a good reason to let it play out. However, if you already have the information you need about the nature of the couple's conflict, have a sense of their communication style, and see the pattern about to repeat itself again, the time may be perfect. Call a halt to their exchange and tell them that this is a perfect opportunity to teach them a new way to communicate.

Take your Talking Stick out of the drawer, off the shelf, out from underneath the sofa or wherever, and hold it ceremoniously as you explain. (A detailed description of a Talking Stick follows in the "Materials" section.) I tell the couple that this technique is borrowed from the wisdom of Native Americans and is very ancient.

The premise is that in conversation, we must learn to take turns. So often, misunderstanding occurs because we don't listen to one another. We are so busy formulating our response to what we *assume* the other person is saying, that we don't really hear what is said. This exercise helps people get accustomed to really listening to one another; even more, it helps each person understand the other's perspective. Many times, when each partner understands the perspective of the other, the conflict is transformed, and options that lead to resolution become available.

I always predict that this exercise will feel phony and orchestrated at first. Encourage your couple to trust the process, and tell them that it has been helpful to many people who have problems communicating with each other.

There are two roles to be played in this technique: (a) asking questions and listening, and (b) expressing feelings or perceptions. The number-one rule is that only the person holding the Talking Stick may express feelings or perceptions. The other person must listen carefully until the one holding the stick is finished. The person listening may ask questions in order to clarify what was said, but the only questions that may be asked are those that elicit information about the perspective of the one talking. The one listening then tests to be sure that he or she understands the perspective of the other. This is done by stating the position/perspective back to the one talking in the listener's own words. Suggest using an opening phrase such as, "I hear you saying . . . ," or "I think what you mean is . . . ," or "You are saying that. . . ." If the person holding the stick agrees that he or she has been understood, the stick is handed to the listener, and the roles reverse. But if the one talking has not been understood, he or she corrects the misperception. Again, the listener checks to be sure the message is clear: "So what you're saying is. . . ." Once understanding is accomplished, the stick is transferred.

I tell the couple that the most difficult role is the role of the listener-learner. That person is asked to put his or her perspective on the back burner and concentrate on the perspective of the other. Emphasize that *understanding* the other does not imply *agreement with* the other. Also emphasize that each person has a chance to explain his or her perspective.

The therapist's role in this technique is that of a benevolent coach. I tell my couple that and say that because the role of the listener-learner is the most difficult, I'll start by helping that person. Then, I hand the Talking Stick to one of them and swing over to sit closer to the listener-learner. (These days, I use an office chair that swivels and rolls.)

Coaching is an art, but you will do fine if you are brave enough to interrupt and empathic enough to be kind and supportive. The listener-learner may not know what question to ask in order to get started. Help him or her by returning to the argument you interrupted in the first place. Prompt the listener-learner by reminding him or her of what that scenario was. You may need to take the lead by posing the first question, "Monica, how did you feel when . . . ?"

If the listener-learner is having trouble thinking of what to ask, sometimes I'll enter into a "private" conversation with him or her. I might say something like "Mike, I was wondering whether or not Monica meant she was angry or sad about your comment. Do you know?" If Mike thinks he knows, ask him to check it out with Monica. If he doesn't know, invite him to ask her. Remember, his job is to collect all the information he can in order to understand, not agree with, her perspective.

As therapists, we know that one of the greatest gifts we have is the ability to ask the right questions. We also know how difficult that is. In this technique, we're asking our clients to do that very thing; ask each other the right questions. If we help them improve their skills in asking the right questions, we have been good coaches indeed.

If the person with the Talking Stick generally has trouble expressing him- or herself anyway, the task of holding the stick and expressing feelings openly may seem overwhelming. In that case, I'll swing around to that person and coach. This is more a supportive gesture than anything else. Sometimes, I'll whisper, "Good job!" or "Nicely done!"—something simple that might encourage more of the same (self-disclosure).

Before it's all over, you will be coaching back and forth, correcting the listener-learner's questions or helping to develop them, and/or encouraging the person with the Talking Stick.

Your clients will try every trick in the book to make the case that they have the real truth of the matter, not because they are devious or ill-intentioned, but because they want to win at this and to point out to their partner, and to their therapist, that they are right. Therefore, you'll get questions from the listener-learner like the following: "You tell me why I said that to you; hadn't you just spouted off to me in a sarcastic tone of voice?" You have to jump in and point out that the question is out of bounds because it is not really an attempt to clarify the speaker's perspective.

Once a couple has used the technique with you, encourage them to practice it at home. Although you may never make it the focus of your work with them, you can always revisit the process when the occasion presents itself in session.

That's all there is to it. The Talking Stick serves as a tangible sign of who does what for a given period of time. The one holding the stick expresses his or her perception of and feelings about the situation or event. The one listening and learning waits until the other has finished, then asks as many questions as necessary until he or she clearly understands the perspective and feelings of the one talking. That accomplished, the Talking Stick is handed over to the listener-learner, and the roles reverse.

Materials

For a number of years, I did not have a real Talking Stick. I had seen a few in Colorado. My husband and I have vacationed in the mountains for years. When we are in resort areas, we sometimes wander in and out of shops and galleries. I had seen a Talking Stick or two in places that specialize in southwestern and Native American art. They were lovely works of art and quite expensive. The wooden sticks were sanded smooth and decorated with feathers and leather tongs. Some have beadwork on them as well.

The Talking Stick I used was a far cry from the beautiful objects just described, but it worked fine. It was an acrylic wand filled with colored liquid in which sparkly stars and glitter float. I got it at a specialty gift shop at the local mall; teenagers tend to frequent the place.

Then, on a recent trip to Colorado to meet with Jack, my therapist-artist friend who did the illustrations for this book, I discovered affordable Talking Sticks at an antique store just down the street from his office. The selection of lovely Talking Sticks were made by Navajo Americans

and were about $30. I am happy to share this recent source: Junk-Tique, Inc., 313 Main St., Frisco, Colorado, 80443, phone: 970-668-3040.

Feel free to be creative and use whatever you want for your Talking Stick. You may even want to let your creative juices flow and make your own!

Practice Example

I return to Lydia and Sam, the couple with whom I first used the technique. Although Lydia was familiar with the concept, she had never practiced the technique; therefore, it was a new behavior to her.

"I don't get any real help from you with the kids! You walk in at the end of the day all sweetness and light. The kids think you're Mr. Disneyland Dad! I need you to help me! It's like I'm doing this all by myself!" Lydia lamented with no small amount of anger.

"You're starting on me again! I'm sick of you always blaming me! I work my ass off for this family and nobody even notices!"

We were off and running with the thematic conflict. I stopped them at this point and explained the Talking Stick technique. I suggested we start by giving the stick to Lydia because she began the conversation. When she did not resume talking spontaneously, I asked Sam what he would like to ask her. He looked at me helplessly. "To get started in this, maybe you could ask her more about how she feels," I offered.

"OK, so how do you feel?" he dutifully responded, with undeniable sarcasm in his voice.

Ignoring his attitude, she said, "I feel like you don't give one damn about me! It doesn't matter to you what my day is like! Since you do the work that makes the money, I don't count! You think you do your part because you have the job. I'm the only one who takes care of everything that happens at home! You think you don't have any responsibility to discipline the kids; that's my job. It's not fair! These kids need two parents! Sometimes, I feel like I might as well be a single parent!"

"Wait a minute, now, I do more stuff with my kids than most . . ." began Sam's reply.

I interrupted. "That's against the rules, Sam. Your job is to understand how Lydia feels. In a minute, you'll get a turn to express your feelings, but right now, only Lydia gets to tell how she feels. Remember, you don't have to agree, you only have to understand." In the silence that followed, Sam turned to me with a blank look on his face. "Now what?" he asked.

"Well, do you think you understand what she just expressed?"

"Yeah, I think so."

"Why don't you check that out with her; see if you really do understand."

Focusing his attention on his wife, Sam said, "Well, you think that I'm a bad father, that I don't take care of the kids like I should."

"No!" Lydia responded, shaking her head and scooting forward in her chair. "You are not a bad father! The kids love you, and it's clear that you love them. This is about *me*. You won't help me with the hard part. You have to discipline kids! I swear, you let them run all over you! You are such a pushover! The kids know it. They can always talk their way around anything with you! If you really cared about *me*, you would help me out and back me up more."

"I simply can't do what I don't think is right!" Sam said rather despondently.

"Wait, wait . . ." I interrupted.

"I know, I know," he acknowledged. "Sorry."

"It seems you are ready to do some talking. Sam, let's see if you understand Lydia's perspective at this point so we can let you have a turn."

"OK. Lydia, you want me to be stricter with the kids and back you up when you punish them."

"Basically, yes," she said.

I suggested Lydia hand the Talking Stick to Sam, and I scooted in my chair to position myself closer to Lydia. "Where would you like to start?" I asked her.

Looking directly at Sam, she said, "Don't you think I have a right to want you to help me?"

Again, I intervened. "That question is not really in the spirit of trying to understand Sam's perspective. Could you take another direction?" Silence ensued. "Lydia, do you know what Sam meant when he said something about not being able to do what he doesn't think is right?"

"Not really."

"Why don't you ask him about that."

"What did you mean by that?" she queried.

"Lydia, it's about your temper. You are so hard on those kids. You don't give them an inch of breathing room. A lot of times, I feel like I have to soften up with them because you are so angry."

That conversation marked a turning point in the direction of our work. Sam talked about his frustration with Lydia's prevailing anger and angst. He saw her as overreacting to the kids' behavior because of her own unhappiness. Over the years, he came to feel that nothing he did would ever be enough to make her happy. He had tried to express his concern about this, but every attempt at conversation ended in a conflict. Lydia would become defensive, accuse him of attacking her, and then blame him for being mean and abusive. After several such episodes, Sam retreated, vowing not to venture into the dangerous waters again. Instead, he did everything he could to "make up for" Lydia's harsh (in his mind) treatment of the children quietly, as he said, "kind of on the sly."

Lydia confessed that she was generally unhappy, mostly because of her insecurity about Sam's affection for her. She was nagged by the notion that, eventually, he would tire of her and move on. She was always looking for signs of his loyalty, or lack thereof. In her mind, if he would support her in her parenting of the children, especially the discipline, she would know that he was really "with her."

We continued to use the Talking Stick technique episodically in therapy. It was invaluable in breaking through the defensive structures that had so restricted their communication.

A Soulful Relationship
Nurturing the Mythical, Magical Images of Love

Part of healing a wounded relationship, or creating stronger ties in a loosely knit one, is the communication of matters deeply personal. As therapists working with couples trying to heal the wound or bridge the gap between them, our job is to provide opportunities in which they can express the essence of their affection for one another.

The expression of deeply held feelings is a stumbling block for many of the people who seek our help. I think it is important to offer opportunities for expression that go beyond the speaking/writing mode. This tool taps into the creative/artistic resources of just about anyone. (Note: This tool is effective in individual therapy as well. The second practice example illustrates its use with individual clients.)

Materials

Present the couple with two disposable cameras. If you can't find cameras with fewer than 24 exposures, give the couple one camera to share. Although this is a relative financial burden for the therapist, I think it is well worth it. The cameras are not that costly, and there is something about presenting cameras to the clients that honors the assignment and underscores the importance of the task you are about to propose. If it is impossible for you to incur the cost, or you have ethical reservations about it (perhaps you will perceive the method as giving clients a gift), so be it; they can buy their own.

Instructions

Tell your clients that you want them to collect images of how they feel about the other, and about their relationship. Their pictures can be of anything—still life, nature, people, anything that conveys a feeling about the other and/or a sense of the relationship. If it seems advisable, cue your clients a little by suggesting various emotions/sentiments to capture, such as longing, sensitivity, commitment, loyalty, lust/desire, sweetness, fidelity, joy, strength, uncertainty, adoration, warmth, friendship, devotion, love, rapture, concern, romance, and so on. I keep a list of these words in my "handouts" file, and on occasion, I give each person a copy.

Selecting and taking the photos should be a private experience for both. They are not to take their pictures in the company of the other or talk about their pictures to the other. If they are using one camera, one partner takes the first half and the other partner takes the remaining exposures. I have found that 10 or 12 photos may be a bit much for some people. It may be that what they need to convey can be expressed with three or four pictures. Tell your clients that the number of pictures is not really important. What is important is that they express what they need to express.

When the film is developed, both partners go through their own pictures, writing descriptive words or phrases on the back that explain the emotions/sentiments represented. (This not only documents the intent of the photo, but also provides practice in attaching emotions to words.)

At the appointed session, each person shares the pictures he or she took with his or her partner. The sharing of the pictures, and the communication that accompanies the experience, should be a positive experience for your couple. You hope that you have enabled them to express themselves to each other in new ways.

Practice Examples

Ted and Kate sought therapy when the success of their marriage appeared doomed. Ted had moved out 3 months ago, and Kate had started packing boxes for the permanent split that appeared inevitable. It was the second marriage for both; Ted had three grown children, and Kate had a teenage daughter.

In my experience of working with people in second or third or fourth marriages, the other person's children are the greatest source of conflict. The case of Ted and Kate was no exception.

Ted's family was a closed system. It was almost impossible to get in and just as difficult to get out. Newcomers to the family were held at arm's length for a long time before entrance was granted. Ted's younger brother's wife (also a second marriage) got in only after producing a child, 3 years after their marriage. Ted and Kate would not have children together, which added to the debit side of her ranking.

Ted's tightly knit family lived in close approximation, in a collection of homes on what was once the family farm. Ted's father had inherited the property from his father, who had farmed it like his father before him. Ted's father was more interested in building than in farming, and he subdivided the farm for residential development, leaving a portion of select acreage for the family. Ted and his first wife built a home on the property, as did his father and mother and, later, his brother. Ted's son built on the property shortly after he married, and Ted's daughter received a building site 3 years ago as a wedding present. When Ted and Kate married (shortly after his daughter's wedding), Kate moved into his house.

Kate had grown up in a distant state and moved to the area with her first husband, who was transferred by his company. Kate had a good relationship with her parents and two brothers, although distance made their personal visits infrequent. When she divorced, Kate decided to stay in the city she now called home; she had good friends and a good job, and her daughter was happy and doing well in school.

When Ted and Kate met, it was love at first sight. They had a whirlwind romance and married only months after they met, feeling secure in their feelings for each other because, as Ted said, "At our age, we knew what we wanted, and we knew it when we saw it!" Within 5 months of the marriage, all hell broke loose.

Ted's children, Janie and Brent, made Kate's life impossible. Their disdain for her was scarcely veiled. They flaunted their position as the rightful heirs and made sure she knew it. They were suspicious of Kate's true affection for their father and suspected that she was attracted more to his money than to him.

They continued to use their father's home as their own even after he and Kate married. They came over to swim, borrow tools and equipment, or just hang out. At first, Kate exhausted herself trying to please and appease them.

Ted, on the other hand, was jealous of the relationship between Kate and her ex-husband. They spoke frequently on the phone about their daughter, and they met occasionally to attend school functions, dance recitals, or family events such as weddings and funerals. Ted saw this as excessive encounters for divorced parents. He wondered what it meant.

The couple attended therapy sessions regularly for more than a year, but very little had actually changed. Kate continued to think that Ted's relationship with his family was "sick," and she believed that his real priority was his children and their mother, rather than her. For his part, Ted doubted the depth of her affection. He had a nagging suspicion that when the chips were down, she would leave him.

Janie and Brent continued to treat Kate poorly, either ignoring her or talking about her behind her back. They dropped in whenever they pleased and treated Kate, as she saw it, "like the hired help." When Janie saw her at the fitness center and reported to her father that Kate was flirting with a male member, Kate, furious, drew a line in the sand. She would no longer subject herself to the children's rejection and rude behavior. Although she encouraged Ted to do whatever he needed to do to have a good relationship with his son and daughter, she would not be involved. If they came over to swim or have a meal, she would leave. If family events were planned, she would not attend.

Ted was flabbergasted. To him, it was a sure sign that she did not really love him. If she was drawing a line, he was, too; no more contact with her ex-husband, period.

Even though the battle lines were drawn, this couple had a deep affection for one another. Neither wanted to give up on the marriage. In sessions, they repeatedly assured each other and me that they wanted to give their commitment every chance. Therapy went on.

In a few months, the rigidity that defined their ultimatums begin to soften. I helped Ted see that Kate's decision not to be around Janie or Brent was necessary for her right now, maybe even a survival tactic. My support of her decision allowed Kate to soften and reconsider. She began to muse about options. When she was ready, and if the kids' behavior improved, and if Ted stood up to them on her behalf now and then, she could imagine things differently.

I was able to challenge Ted's position on Kate having no contact with her ex-husband by appealing to his own parenting. Could he really not see that Kate's daughter deserved the cooperation and positive regard that her parents held for one another? His children had that. Yes, he could see that. We began to talk about what Kate could do to make Ted feel safe when she had contact with her ex-husband.

When some positive movement was under way, I presented a camera to the couple and made the picture assignment. Two weeks later, they came to session with their homework completed.

Ted's pictures were about community. There was a picture of the swimming pool, a gathering place for the clan ever since it was built more than 20 years ago. There was a picture of a display of framed photos on a bookshelf in his study at home. The photos were of family members (from both sides of the family, his *and* Kate's) in a variety of poses and situations. A picture of him and Kate on their wedding day was among them. There was a picture of a flock of Canadian geese swimming in the lake. "I like to think of us like these geese, surrounded by a loving family." He had captured the image of a beautiful monarch butterfly on the butterfly bush in their yard. "When I met Kate, my garden was already grown, so to speak. I was older. I had my business, my friends, my family; but I didn't have her. Like this butterfly, she is the most beautiful thing in the garden. I still can't believe my garden attracted her." These images helped Kate see that Ted's sense of family included her. The importance of family was so ingrained in him that the lens through which he viewed the world was colored by images of family.

Kate's pictures were all about solitude, isolation, and separateness. She had a picture of a nearby lake where they spent weekends on occasion. "When it's just the two of us at the lake, you are a different person. You relax, you read, and we talk a lot. I love having dinner just with you instead of with our usual group of friends that we can't seem to escape. I like being away from your family, too." She also had a picture of a boat anchor with its chain. "See what a unit this is. I want to be a unit like this with you. I saw you as my anchor when we got married, then something happened, and I lost that feeling. I want it back." She had a picture of two leaves floating on serene water. "That. I want us to be that," she said quietly. Ted finally seemed to understand that Kate wasn't going anyplace. All her dreams were of the two of them together.

The climate of the session was transformed. Both had shared visions with the other that were powerful and loving and intimate, although quite different. I used the moment to suggest that they could have it all. Neither asked for something to which the other was opposed; it was just a matter of balance. What could they do, I queried, to have it all?

Before the session was over, they had come up with an idea. They could build a cabin at the lake. Nothing fancy, just a place of their own; a getaway place where life was simple. Kate felt no sense of place. The house in which they lived had been built for another wife. It was Grand Central Station to family and extended family. If they had a place of their own, she could tolerate life on the "compound." Ted liked the idea but was nervous. What if his kids wanted to use the cabin? With Kate's emphatic "No way!" he turned to me pleadingly. I assured him that he and Kate had every right to a place that was just theirs; visitors allowed only by invitation. Acknowledging that, emotionally, it would be a difficult stretch for him to deny access to his family, Ted agreed that Kate's need for privacy was the most important consideration.

The couple walked out the door with excitement all over their faces. Maybe they could have it all.

Cindy first started therapy her junior year in college, when she scratched on her arms with a razor blade and told her roommate. Shortly before the suicidal gesture, she had been having panic attacks.

Her level of emotional distress did not exactly make sense for a young woman who had so much going for her. She was from an affluent, middle-class family that was encouraging and supportive. She was intelligent, attractive, and popular. She was a good athlete and was on a tennis scholarship. She was a member of one of the best social sororities on campus and was close to her three suitemates. Nevertheless, she had been anxious and depressed for almost 2 years.

Initially, she was very resistant to therapy. She reluctantly took the antidepressants her doctor prescribed. She was suspicious of therapist-types and often referred to the "spooky" psychiatrist she saw for a short time in elementary school for some school phobia issues. Although a therapist's office was the last place she wanted to be, she understood that it was a necessary part of conquering her condition. "No offense," she said more than once, "but I hate therapists."

Several years later, she was still struggling with anxiety, panic, and depression, and she was still in therapy. There were successes during those years: She bonded with her therapist, graduated from college, got her first job, got her first place, got a dog, overcame her fear of flying in airplanes, and fell in love for the first time. There were trials and tribulations as well: Some days she was too anxious to go to work. Her live-in boyfriend turned out to be problematic; he abused alcohol and was not very good to her. After they broke up, she was hospitalized for cutting on her wrists again.

About a year later, in a time of relative calm, when she was feeling good about herself and her life was working, she met someone else. The someone else was another woman. All the pieces of the puzzle began falling into place. The anxiety and panic made sense in light of a secret so deeply buried that she did not even have access to it.

Years ago, there had been an initial attraction to another female in high school. But the experience was so traumatic to her that she sealed it up, along with its emotional components, and stored it so far from consciousness that she forgot about it. How could it be possible for someone like Cindy to be a lesbian? Her tidy little life would be blown all to hell if her sexual identity were anything but heterosexual.

The only place safe enough to explore a curiosity that Cindy was only vaguely aware of was on the Internet. Almost unintentionally, she found herself seeking out sites frequented by gays and lesbians. She became less and less invested in life around her and more and more compelled to explore the secret unfolding in chat rooms.

She was able to tell me about her new obsession with the Internet, but she was unable to reveal what she was really doing. It was only when she made plans to meet with the woman with whom she had been communicating for several months that she hinted at what was going on. Finally, after their meeting, she told me.

Although I was not aware of why Cindy was changing, her transformation had been apparent to me. Her affect was more positive; she even looked different. Her eyes were brighter, and she laughed and smiled more often. She seemed more confident about her job, her relationship with her parents, everything. I attributed it to the evolutionary process of therapy. Although I was missing a huge piece, in a way, I was right. Cindy was becoming strong and healthy enough to be who she was. Meeting Barbara was a natural next step.

Cindy struggled in her attempts to talk to me about Barbara. Although accepting, I was a straight woman, and it was hard for her to find the courage to talk about her feelings for another woman. However, as her therapist, I was the only person in her life with whom she could share this evolving story. I thought the camera exercise might be a safe way for her to tell me about what was happening to her. It was.

Her photographs spoke volumes. She had gone to a Japanese garden to take her pictures.

One photo was of a woolly worm because "it was the closest thing I could find to a cocoon!" She also took a picture of a butterfly. Placing the two pictures side by side, she said, "This is what has been happening to me. See, I was trapped in this little tight wrap; getting out has been a huge struggle. But look at me now! I'm big and beautiful and free!"

She also had several pictures of a lovely pond; in one picture, the water was calm and serene. She explained that like the pond, she appeared calm and serene on the surface. However, there was a whole world teeming below the surface that nobody could see. It was her secret world, and the real essence of who she was lived there. For the next picture, she threw a stone into the water and captured the ripples it made. The ripples symbolized how this one small piece of her life had such a huge impact on everything else. She also had a picture of her new girlfriend, which she presented proudly. She watched my face expectantly, as one does when hoping for affirmation.

The pictures allowed Cindy to express her feelings in a way that felt safer than direct conversation. With the pictures doing the talking, she could be less worried about overexposing herself or finding the right words to express what she was feeling.

PART IV

Measuring Tape, Levels, and Plumbs

Tools for Special Projects

Finding a Safe Place

This tool is useful in situations where anxiety is a prevailing theme for your client. Although medication is standard in treating anxiety, it is seldom enough in the long run. Also, there are those clients who resist or refuse medication for a variety of reasons. This technique is a nice alternative or addition to appropriate medication and talk therapy. Although a guided imagery tool, it offers a bit of a different twist. It differs from the process in Chapter 4, "Discovering the Inner Child," in that your clients will be responding to you verbally as you move through the technique.

Instructions

Tell your clients that this exercise involves relaxation and guided imagery. During the guided imagery, you will be asking them to respond to your questions out loud (as opposed to remaining silent as mental images are created).

Then, take your clients through a basic relaxation process, either your own or the one found in Chapter 4.

When the relaxation process is complete, instruct your clients to keep their eyes closed during the guided imagery. Ask them to think about a place where they once felt safe. It might be a place from childhood, or perhaps a place that was visited during adulthood. It could even be a place in their imagination.

Some people will conjure up such a place immediately; others may need several minutes to locate their place. You can usually tell by the expression on their face when they locate their place (even with eyes closed). I usually say, "Have you found it yet?"

When your clients indicate that they have it, ask them to tell you where it is. Then, ask them to tell you all about it. What does it look like? Encourage them to be as specific as possible. When did they go there?

How does it smell? How did they feel there? What other memories do they have associated with this place? Be exhaustive in your questions so that your clients are pushed to recall all of the images of their safe place that they possibly can.

When you have thoroughly explored the image and the history of it, tell your clients that the safe place is still available to them; they can revisit that place of comfort and solace in their mind's eye. All they have to do is conjure up the image as they have just done. Evoking the sense of safety and protection once felt in the safe place may be enough to get the jitters under control, allow an intentional shift of emotions from nervous to calm, or even avoid a panic attack. Suggest that your clients practice the technique and report the results in the next session.

Practice Example

I was not the first therapist to work with Evelyn. She had seen others over the course of many years. She was not a therapist-shopper; her other courses of therapy lasted more than a year or two each. It appeared that she had worked hard in therapy, and she reported that she was much improved from the way she was when it all started.

Evelyn suffered from anxiety and panic. She was diagnosed with major depression and posttraumatic stress disorder, and she was being followed by a psychiatrist for maintenance medication. She came to me because old symptoms were returning. Chief among them was generalized anxiety and the compulsion to burn herself on the oven or with an iron. She was also beginning to have night terrors again, a symptom that had been under control for several years.

Given the level of trauma in her history, Evelyn functioned at quite a high level. She was married to a devoted husband and had a grown son. She was a homemaker who was active in her church and volunteered at the community food pantry. She and her husband belonged to a country club and played in the couple's golf league. She also was a member of a bridge group and book club. Only her closest friends were aware of her secret illness.

Evelyn was the first-born child in her family and had a brother 9 years younger than she. Her mother had been severely disturbed for as long as she could remember. Her mother seldom left the house, and when the demands of cooking and cleaning were satisfied, she sat in a rocking chair by a window and rocked by the hour. Evelyn realized over time that her once lively and lovely mother was struck with what we now call postpartum depression, although at the time, it was a misunderstood malady. Neighbor women whispered about the strange lady down the block who never joined them for coffee or participated in PTA and was seldom seen outside the house.

Evelyn's life at home revolved around not upsetting her mother. She worried about her all the time and did whatever she could to make her mother happy. She was mature beyond her years; she helped with her younger brother, cleaned, cooked, and waited on her mother while other girls were playing dolls together and having lemonade stands in their front yards.

Evelyn's father doted on his wife. He ministered tirelessly to his dismal spouse, always hopeful that her sadness would eventually go away.

Evelyn and her brother attended parochial school from kindergarten through senior high. The school was owned by the Catholic Church and operated by nuns. Evelyn was certain that something horrible had happened to her at the school in the third grade, because in nightmares and daytime visions, she saw the small high window in the girls' restroom. She remembered the green and white tiles of the bathroom floor and could feel the coldness of them against her back. In an effort to recapture the rest of the bathroom memories, Evelyn made a pilgrimage back to the school of her nightmares. The bathroom was exactly as she remembered it, with the high window, green and white tiles and all. But she was unsuccessful in reclaiming any more recollection; the images that haunted her remained a mystery.

I thought that helping her discover a safe place in her imagination might help her feel less terrorized when symptoms of panic and compulsion occurred. After the guided relaxation, she discovered her safe place without any trouble. When she was a small girl, she spent most of each summer with her grandmother, who lived on a farm outside a small Kansas community. Evelyn loved her summers with her grandmother, whom she described as a big-breasted woman who always wore an apron. Grandmother was loving and soft and attentive. She smelled of homemade bread and took time to read to her granddaughter every evening on the porch swing.

By the side of the house was a mulberry bush, its branches arching to the ground, creating a circle of graceful leaves and dark purple berries that rivaled a queen's best ballgown. Beneath the elegant skirt, a small girl could create a haven of enchantment. It was a cool and peaceful escape from the blazing summer sun. Underneath the skirt's leafy folds, the muted sunlight created a friendly and mysterious atmosphere. Evelyn took her dolls and all their accessories to her special place. There were beds and buggies to make and tea parties and weddings to attend; it was always busy under the mulberry bush. Sometimes, her grandmother brought a glass of ice-cold milk and ginger cookies to add to the festivities. It was a place where Evelyn felt safe and loved and happy.

Evelyn's joy when recalling her mulberry bush retreat was evident on her beaming face. I pushed for as many specific recollections as she could conjure—taste, touch, sight, smell, and sound—because all of them help in creating a powerful image. She remembered the feel of the dirt and its smell and its color. She talked of smashing the purple berries to use as food for her dolls and of sticking whole ones in her dolls' hair for adornment. Sometimes, she could hear her grandfather and his helper talking on the porch about the weather or the crops or the baseball game. She was invisible, safe, and secure.

Evelyn practiced using the image of her safe place when the feelings of anxiety that lived in some deep place below consciousness surfaced to the top like an air bubble. The technique was not a definitive defense against the serious psychological consequences of early trauma, but it was something I could offer and something she could do. One small tool can make a difference.

Thin Places
A Way to Talk About God

As a mental health professional, I am amazed by the number of brochures announcing upcoming seminars and conferences on the themes of "psychology and spirituality" that come across my desk. And when I thumb through the pages of my professional journals, I often find a study on the influence or importance of religion on the subjects' lives, be they college students, racial minorities, or nursing home residents. Bookstores are replete with new tomes on every aspect of spirituality, from new ideas about ancient religions to New Age systems of belief. New journals on spirituality and health are popping up everywhere. Perhaps this phenomenon of a new interest in religion is a result of the cyclical nature of things, or maybe it is a new awareness that technology doesn't hold the keys to happiness after all. Whatever the reasons, interest in the spiritual life is keen.

It seems clear that if we as therapists ignore the spiritual lives of our clients, we are not seeing the whole picture. How do we provide an opportunity for our clients to talk about this important and sensitive part of their lives? How do we invite them to share their deeply held religious values and perspectives? How can we provide counsel and offer support, even when their beliefs may be a far cry from our own?

Although the following technique is not *the* answer, it may be *an* answer. It is, at least, a place to start.

Instructions

I start this session by reminding my clients that I am interested in every aspect of their lives. Sometimes, I'll remind them that we have been talking about the emotional, social, physical, financial, legal, or sexual aspect, but that we have not yet discussed their spiritual/religious life. Sometimes, that's as far as you'll get. Your clients may end the process right there by declaring that there is no religious/spiritual component to their life. So be it. I honor that perspective like any other. I will explore that if I can by asking why there is not such an aspect to their lives. How did it happen that they do not see themselves as religious/spiritual? That can turn out to be an interesting and important story.

I have had clients whose parents never introduced them to the realm of the spirit in any way. Some are bitter about that and harbor a seething resentment. Others say that their parents crammed the whole religious thing down their throats until escape from anything resembling religion became a pressing life goal. Some have had heartfelt disappointments in their faith lives in the past and have abandoned their beliefs. Others felt that they could never live up to the expectations of their religious convictions, so they removed themselves from a painful sense of inadequacy by leaving it all behind. These stories are invaluable. They give you the chance to accept, validate, and sometimes challenge your client's perceptions.

On the other hand, if you find that your client does have a religious/ spiritual perspective, you are ready to introduce the Thin Places technique. Thin Places will work with any faith tradition because the client determines the content of his or her work. Sometimes, I ask my clients to do the work in session, and other times, I assign this as homework.

I usually say something like the following, but every therapist using the manual will have his or her own way of delivering the instructions.

The ancient Celts conquered much of the known world before the Romans ruled. They were fierce warriors who terrified enemies by going into battle naked, screaming blood-curdling war cries. In peacetime, they were an agrarian people with a deep respect for the land.

The Celts were pagans who had a sense of wonder and awe for the stamp of divinity in all things natural. They believed that the supernatural invades all of life, and they recognized no split between the sacred and the secular.

The Celts believed that there were special physical places and special occasions when the barrier between this world and otherworldly events and beings became more permeable than in ordinary places and occasions. They called such places or events "thin places."

I was wondering if you have ever experienced such a phenomenon in your life. It would be a time when the divine was close at hand, a time when the presence of God was almost tangible. It might be an experience from childhood; it might be something that occurred yesterday.

Invite your client to express that encounter by drawing it. If you want the work to be done in your office, provide large paper, like a sketch pad or drawing pad, and colored markers. Encourage your client to be as creative as possible. Suggest that symbolic representation of the event might make it easier to draw if he or she appears overwhelmed or intimidated by the thought of drawing.

When the client is finished, ask him or her to tell the story that goes with the drawing.

Materials

- Large drawing paper
- Colored markers

Practice Example

Demetrios was a young man in his late 20s who sought therapy because "his life just wasn't working." He was a college graduate, and he worked as an insurance adjuster. He desperately wanted to get married, but he did not have a girlfriend; in fact, he had never had a girlfriend. He also felt isolated from a community of peers. Everyone at his workplace was either older or, if closer to his age, married and too busy to include him. He had never had a close community of peers, he confessed. All his life, he was on the outside and never felt a sense of belonging. Basically, he saw himself as a social failure.

This young man's issues with relationships were not hard to imagine because it was hard for me to have a relationship with him. To say he did not have the gift of gab would be a colossal understatement. Our sessions were difficult and exhausting for both of us. But when I explained that if he could learn to have a satisfying relationship with his therapist, he would be better able to have a satisfying relationship with anyone, he signed on. As the weeks went by, I had pretty much pulled out all my tricks and techniques in an effort to somehow keep the ball rolling. One day, I thought of the Thin Places tool. Trust me, I had him do this in session! I was glad to have something to use up our grueling minutes together.

He drew a picture of an experience at church camp when he was 13 years old. The sky was blue, the grass was green, and there were smiling kids all around, including him! He remembered feeling that life was good and God was present that summer. He remembered feeling a part of things. He remembered feeling liked by others.

He had drifted far from that place of happiness, but now it was pulled to consciousness. I asked him what church he attended these days. He confessed that he had not established a church home since moving out of his parents' house and living on his own. Maybe reconnecting to the church and faith of his adolescence would be at least one path to the life he desired. He left the office with a new idea and a new direction.

20

Enmeshment
Deconstructing the Net

Therapists wear many hats. Depending on the circumstance, we are coaches, advisors, consultants, mentors, referees, tribal elders, mediators, spiritual directors, and paid companions. In this technique, the therapist is a teacher.

Enmeshment is one of the most common and complicating dynamics of the human condition. The phenomenon occurs in the most well-meaning people with the best of intentions. Not only is it indicative of individual personality constructs, but it also reflects many cultural influences, including gender stereotypes, parenting models, intimacy myths, and religious teachings.

When I talk about enmeshment, I am not talking about the mutually beneficial relationship that occurs when human beings need each other. Nor do I think independence should be valued above all as a sign of health, and dependence on others devalued. To me, enmeshment reflects personal boundaries that are so ill-defined that they cause distress in the relationship.

It seems true that good fences really do make good neighbors. If the fence between the properties of neighbors is well constructed, the neighbors get along well. They can lean on it and have a chat, or climb over it when desired or necessary; they might even crawl through on occasion. However, if the fence breaks down and the livestock of one neighbor meanders over to another's property and begins to graze, trouble begins.

Although there are as many examples of enmeshed relationships as there are people in them, two prototypical models come to mind. Model 1 is the couple that is in constant conflict, or complains of feeling out of touch with each other. Earlier in their relationship, they were inseparable. They loved to do all the same things, liked the same music, the same movies. Now, they can't even agree on a restaurant. "We are just so distant!" they lament. In reality, they may be much too close.

Model 2 is the mother and her high school daughter who appear in the therapist's office when the girl is a junior or senior in high school. Historically so close, the distraught mother now reports that she doesn't know what has happened. She doesn't know her child anymore, they fight all the time, and she's discovered that her heretofore ideal daughter is keeping secrets about where she goes, who she is with, what she is doing, and so on. She has been caught telling lies. The mother is frantic that something is terribly wrong. Actually, mother and daughter may be too close, and the closeness threatens the daughter's plans to attend college next year. She has to find some way to "break up" with the mother who has been such a constant presence in her life.

Enmeshment may not be difficult for the therapist to identify, but dealing with it is another story. I developed this model as a way to educate clients about the net in which they are caught. When people understand the concept of enmeshment, the battle is half-won. I use this in individual therapy, couples therapy, and family therapy regularly. I have also used it many times in the public speaking arena when addressing topics on relationships and intimacy. People seem to get it. I hope you will find it helpful.

Instructions

The visual demonstration of this teaching technique to your clients is the most important part. I have found that people may not remember exactly what you said about enmeshment, but they do remember how you represented it; thus, the drawings.

I begin by describing and naming the syndrome. Most people feel some degree of relief when their condition has a name. For example, when one makes an appointment with the doctor because of weight loss, extreme thirst, frequent urination, an insatiable appetite, and general malaise, one is anxious because the symptoms are frightening. What could this mean? Cancer? The doctor takes some blood and some urine and diagnoses diabetes. What relief! Diabetes is not a good thing to have, but naming the disease normalizes the patient's symptoms because everybody knows about diabetes. It is treatable and doesn't have to be life-threatening.

People in intimate relationships who are in conflict or disharmony are anxious. What does this mean? Tell them you think you know what this means—they are enmeshed. Then you say something like, "This is very common!" or "I see this all the time." Now, your couple feels a little better. Most people don't understand the word, but you now have their full attention.

Here is what I say to my clients; you will have your own way of expressing the material:

Enmeshment happens to good people in good relationships for good reasons. It is the result of a desire to be very close with the other. In fact, enmeshment occurs only in intimate relationships. Let's look at what happens in a relationship between two people who are close. [I use a man and a woman if I am working with a heterosexual couple, a parent and child if that is the case, etc. For purposes of illustration here, I'll use a man and woman.] So, here is our couple. Let's say the woman is my right hand, and the man is my left hand.

These two, quite separate individuals find each other in life somehow and are mutually attracted to each other. Eventually, they come together in a place of closeness that we call "intimacy." [Slowly bring hands together.]

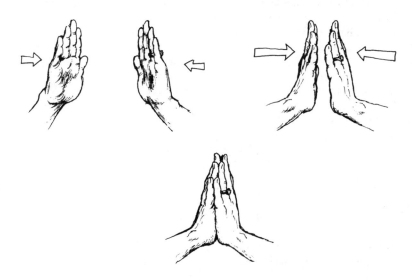

Intimacy means "of a close and personal nature." This may or may not include sexual relations. But for our purposes now, we have a man and woman who are very close, so let's say it does involve sex.

As human beings, we are driven to this place of closeness. It is one of life's greatest joys and pleasures. It is a place of oneness. We love it!

However, we can't stay there very long. Some innate sense kicks in, and we are drawn back to our separate place, our place of individuality. [Move hands apart.]

In the case of our couple here, let's say the woman [indicate with right hand] has her own activities, interests, and relationships. She has a job and has friends at work, she loves to garden and is crazy about the theater. She has a good relationship with her family of origin and talks to her sister every week.

Likewise, this man [indicate with left hand] has his own life. He has his work that involves some traveling, which he enjoys. He plays golf whenever he can and has a weekly foursome. He also enjoys fishing and has a fishing buddy. So, both of these people have quite separate lives.

However, we don't like to be out there alone with our separate lives for very long, and so once again, we are compelled to bridge the distance and return to that place of closeness and intimacy.

Now, we have created the picture of healthy intimacy; it is a coming together for closeness or oneness and a moving apart for separateness or individuality, over and over. [Move your hands together and apart as if clapping. In fact, end by clapping and say something like, "See how easily this works; it's healthy intimacy and it should be celebrated!"]

When enmeshment occurs, this process gets all messed up. It happens when, at the close and intimate phase, this occurs:

You see, in healthy intimacy, when the two individuals come together as one, each individual is still clearly separate. But when this happens [look at hands], that boundary is lost. Now, it's hard to tell just who is who and what is what!

This occurs when, for example, this woman [leaving hands in locked position, wiggle fingers of right hand to indicate the woman] comes to believe that she is responsible for this man's happiness, that his well-being, general satisfaction with life, and good mood are her responsibility (when actually they are not).

And for the man [wiggle fingers of left hand], it might be that he feels insecure and uncertain about her affection and fidelity. Therefore, in order to reassure himself that all is well, he wants to know where she is and what she is doing at all times. He may feel it is his duty to manage their relationship as well, and if they are not together, he may feel a loss of control that is disconcerting. Therefore, he calls her on her cell phone to check on her numerous times each day. When she wants to go shopping with girlfriends or spend time with her sister, it may feel as if he's losing her; therefore, he is not supportive of her life apart from him.

Alternatively, you may prefer this example for the man:

Maybe this man here [wiggle fingers of left hand] feels it is his job to fix whatever seems to be causing her distress. When she comes home from work upset because a coworker did not treat her well, he may believe it is his job to fix things, and so he tells her exactly what she should do to remedy the situation. (Actually, that is not his responsibility, and in fact, she does not even want him to fix it, she just wants him to listen to her.)

Now, when these two partners need to separate—perhaps she wants to go to bed because it's been a hard day and she's tired, or he is feeling stressed and grumpy and wants to be alone in his workshop in the garage for a few hours. [At this point pull your hands as if to get them apart, but show that you cannot completely separate them because the fingers are still intertwined.]

What should be a comfortable separation becomes difficult, **and it hurts**. Finally, this happens: [Pulling hard, let your hands fly apart.]

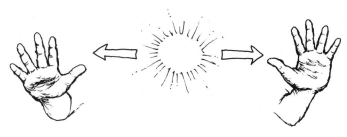

There's an explosion—a fight, an argument, a major conflict. Now, look at how much distance this couple must overcome in order to return to that place of closeness!

The solution is to assist the couple in determining "whose stuff is whose." (I use that phrase because people tend to understand the meaning behind it.) The enmeshment process can be reversed by going back to reclaim each person's boundaries, one at a time.

If the man comes home from work in a grumpy mood, is it really the woman's fault? No. Does she need to help him in his relationships with others so that they will be better and he will be happier? Not unless he asks. Does this man need access to the woman's agenda every day? No. Can he let go of managing the time she spends with girlfriends and relatives? I hope so.

You can help a couple identify the areas in which boundaries are merged or violated and either suggest (if you need to) or mediate other options.

The case of a parent and child is a little different and depends on the age of the child. Parents are responsible for much of their children's lives until the children are developmentally able to assume responsibility themselves. One reason that adolescence is such a trying time is that there are no clear guidelines that tell parents if they are being intrusive in their child's life, or if they are exercising healthy parenting. It's tricky business.

Generally, however, you will recognize the clues. It is good parenting if a parent goes through his or her teen's backpack because there have been changes in behavior and grades that lead the parent to suspect drug use. It is intrusive, however, if a parent routinely goes through a teen's backpack out of curiosity alone.

The following is a list of red flags. If you see examples like these, suspect enmeshment:

- A father is more interested in his son's football than the son is.
- A mother knows all of the relationship issues of her daughter's friends.
- A mother keeps track of her daughter's periods (and there is no medical reason).
- An adolescent daughter calls her mother her best friend.
- A father forces his son to take golf lessons but won't pay for the classes his son wants to take at the art museum.

- The parents of an adolescent go through the tapes in his or her car and remove the ones they don't approve of.
- The parent of a college student phones him or her every day.
- The parents make it clear that their relationship with the children comes before their relationship with each other.

Practice Examples

Terri and Clay, both in their third marriage, owned and operated several convenience stores together. When they separated, they had been married for 4 years; the separation occurred 2 years ago. They were not divorced, nor had divorce proceedings been initiated. They continued to function as husband and wife although they maintained different residences.

Clay made the first therapy appointment for himself. He was certain that Terri had cheated on him, but she would not admit it. He thought he was "losing it" because on one hand, he had what he felt was evidence of her infidelity, but on the other hand, she insisted that she was innocent of wrongdoing and had some pretty convincing arguments herself. He did not know what to believe. Near the end of the first session, he acknowledged that he did not want the marriage to end. He not only still loved Terri, but also depended on her as a business partner. However, he had lost all trust in her and still suspected her of cheating. Terri had already told him that she would do anything it took to save the marriage and was eager to engage in marital counseling. A couples session was scheduled for the following week.

It took only one session to discover that this couple was highly volatile and emotionally intense. In their dysfunctional communication style, he accused, she defended, he clammed up, she badgered, and he exploded. However, threads of affection were woven into the fabric of their relationship right along with the barbed wire.

She was supportive and complimentary of his resolve to quit drinking. It had been a little over 2 years since Clay decided his drinking was out of control and he decided to stop. "AA is not for me," he explained. "I like to take care of things on my own."

Clay praised Terri for the wise business decisions she had made over the course of their marriage. He appreciated her "people skills" as well; everyone liked Terri, and she was a great conversationalist.

Terri and Clay did everything together. Although Terri had had women friends in the past, she rarely got together with them anymore. "Too busy," she said. When Clay had business out of town or went fishing with his brother, he phoned Terri every couple of hours throughout the day. They did not have married friends, or any other resource for interacting with other couples; they did not belong to any social clubs, attend church, or enjoy concerts or the symphony. Neither had a hobby. They did very little reading, but they did watch a lot of TV and enjoyed an occasional movie.

I explained enmeshment to them and told them that they had unrealistic expectations for their relationship. Neither had much of a separate life, so they both looked to the marriage relationship to meet all of their needs. I predicted that the marriage was doomed if they did not untangle themselves from the net in which they were caught. Although they seemed to understand the truth of that, their system was entrenched, and it was very difficult to break free from the pattern. I worked with them individually to try to support/encourage any individual interest I could find. We talked about the benefits of a fitness club, the creative rewards of learning something new in various classes offered in the community, the joy of meeting new people and resurrecting old friendships, and various hobbies or interests that might be pursued. However, no new behaviors were launched. Terri and Clay continued to operate as a single unit, joined at the hip. If Clay became upset over a business issue, Terri did, too, putting his emotionality on as her own and then punishing him for being so reactive. Her criticism flamed the fire of his already aroused temper. The conflict was off and running. When Terri talked to a salesman longer than Clay thought she should, there was hell to pay. He would accuse her of flirting, and she would furiously deny any wrongdoing. Her denial and defensiveness only made him more suspicious.

In the end, this marriage could not be saved. Clay's jealousy and Terri's covert behavior drove the wedge between them even deeper. Their relationship disintegrated into a constant stream of threats and allegations about cheating, infidelity, third parties, and so on.

Several months after they divorced, Clay came to see me again. He wanted me to know that he was seeing a woman and was feeling good about this new relationship. He assured me that this time, he was not going to lose himself. He was being intentional about maintaining his independence. He said that he would not be moving in with this lady, nor would he invite her to move in with him. They were seeing each other five nights a week, with the other two reserved for separate, individual activities. He was seeing more of his daughter (from his first marriage) as well as doing a home improvement project for his mother. Sometimes, people grow and change in therapy even when important relationships are lost.

The Wilkerson family entered therapy because "something has to be done about the chaos in this household!" Marie, the mother, was an English professor at a local university, and Al, the father, was a CPA. They had twin 15-year-old daughters (Rhonda and Randi) and a 12-year-old son (Phillip). Al reported that there was constant conflict in the house. According to him, the source of the conflict was Marie's "high expectations" of everyone. She expected the children to be perfect, and when they were not, she attacked. She also expected him to be the perfect husband, and he wondered if he'd ever be good enough for her. Marie, on the other hand, felt that the source of the conflict was that Al did not put her first. He was more interested in playing golf with Phillip (or coaching his soccer team, according to the season) than he was in spending time with her. He worked long hours in the first place, then wanted to play golf or soccer with Phillip, or watch sports on TV in his free time. That left very little time for her.

Rhonda and Randi agreed that the problem was that their parents would not let them grow up. Phillip said he thought that the real source of the conflict was between the girls in the family, and that he and his dad lived in the eye of the hurricane.

Although there was truth to everyone's perspective, it seemed that the conflict between mother and daughters was closest to the surface, so I began there. First, I saw Marie individually a few times. Next, I saw the girls together once, then each in an individual session. When I brought the women together for a session, I had a much clearer picture. I explained that it appeared that the girls and their mother were enmeshed. I explained enmeshment, pointing out that enmeshed relationships between parents and children were tricky. I applauded Marie's concern and love for her daughters and supported her determination to parent them well.

At this point, I taught the mother and daughters about enmeshment, using examples gleaned from the preceding sessions to illustrate enmeshed behavior.

One example was that Marie periodically picked through the girls' purses or backpacks. If she found personal letters or notes, she read them. She also looked through homework assignments and school papers at will. When the girls discovered yet another invasion of privacy, they would be furious, and a mighty conflict would ensue. Marie justified her behavior because once she had found a note from a girlfriend of Randi's that talked about the girlfriend's sex life. Marie then forbade her daughter to continue to have a relationship with the girl. Another time, a similar event occurred when she discovered what appeared to be a suicide note from one of Rhonda's friends.

The girls were honor students with high academic standing in their high school. For the most part, their friends were good kids with high standards as well. There was no reason for Marie to rummage through their belongings.

Another example of enmeshed behavior was that Marie was intent on listening to conversations the girls had with their friends. She eavesdropped on their telephone conversations and listened outside their bedroom door whenever she could. Recently, when the girls had a sleepover with friends, Marie took a heating vent apart in a bathroom under the room where the girls were gathered so that she could listen to their conversation. The girls discovered her tactics when she forgot to put the cover back in place. Marie also questioned them constantly about their lives—who they saw today, what was said, and so on. Often, she judged what they told her, becoming upset with the information and generally giving advice about how they could have handled the situation better.

In response to this intrusive behavior, the girls had vowed to withhold information about their lives from their mother to punish her. This left Marie feeling pushed away and abandoned.

As it turned out, Al's behavior—staying away from home as often as possible—was the result of the same dynamic. Marie was so intrusive that he fled the house in an attempt to secure some degree of privacy. He made it clear that it was not because of lack of affection for Marie; rather, it was a sense of being engulfed that caused him to seek out activities away from home. Once again, I taught the enmeshment dynamic, this time to Marie and Al.

The family was in therapy for about a year. The thrust of our work was finding a balance between individuation and intimacy. Deconstructing the net that held the family captive to a dysfunctional system of communication and behavior was a tedious but valuable task. It was interesting to discover the ways in which the girls and Al were also players in the enmeshment dynamic. When Marie began disengaging somewhat at home and building a more satisfying life in interests and activities outside the home, Al countered by behaving in ways that would elicit Marie's old behavior. For example, Al once "forgot" to tell Marie that he was going to a political dinner event after golf one Saturday. When he wasn't home at the expected time, she frantically called his business partners, his friends, and then all the area hospitals. When he related this story in session, he overtly complained about her overreaction; however, it seemed pretty clear that he had enjoyed his wife's "meddlesome" and "hysterical" behavior.

Even though the twins understood that their refusal to be more open with their mother about their lives only fueled her intrusive behavior, they clung stubbornly to their resolve to keep their mother out (thus increasing her sense of isolation from them, which in turn elicited her intrusiveness). It was a vicious circle.

In the case of mother and daughters, geography was a good friend of deconstructing the net. When the twins went away to college (out of state), the distance served to help in the process of change. In the case of Al and Marie, as she became more and more interested in cultivating her own interests and activities, he became less and less interested in pursuing activities outside the home.

Rock-Hard Resolve
Holding On

We all encounter those clients whose ability to make decisions and act upon them is not their strong suit. Very unprofessional, judgmental words come to mind: spineless, weak, passive, and wimpy, to name just a few. These are the clients who require a boatload of patience. The "Just Do It!" motto may scream in your head as you once again endure the metaphorical walk down that familiar path that leads to the expected end.

The answer is right there: Get a job! Get a date! Get out (of the job, the marriage, the relationship, the town, the church)! Do something, even if it's wrong!

It's as if the person has lost something. Faith? Confidence? Free will? Choice? Certainly, any sense of personal power has eroded or washed away; maybe it was never there.

Often, these wounded souls have histories of abuse. In those cases, years of therapy may be needed. Sometimes, the inherent lack of ability to take action is part and parcel of a personality disorder, which won't be solved in three to five visits. Occasionally, it is more about a fear so integrated into the psyche that it is not experienced as a fear: Will I lose approval? Will I lose affection? Will I be abandoned? Again, this is not a quick fix.

However, at some point, you will probably help your client unearth a remnant of his or her own strength. You will identify it, clean and polish it a bit, and parade it around as evidence of personal power that dwells just below the surface. At that point, this tool comes in handy.

Instructions

Near the end of a session, present your client with a selection of rocks. I keep mine in an antique wire basket that is in my office as part of the decor. You might want to use a lovely wooden box for your rocks, or a decorative tin or canister. Ask your client to choose a rock to keep. I usually discuss the nature of a rock: It's hard; it holds its shape no matter what; it can be used as a weapon; it can be something you need (if you are building a wall) or something that you need to remove (if you are preparing the soil for a garden). Instruct your client to take his or her rock home and put it someplace where it will be seen often, as a reminder of the rock-hard resolve within. Ask your client to write about the strength that has been discovered and bring what was written to the next session. If you have a client who is resistant to a writing exercise, tell him or her to consider the strength identified and be ready to discuss it in the next session.

Materials

You'll need a selection of rocks, from which your clients can make their choice. See the Materials section in Chapter 13, page 86, on choosing "therapy rocks."

Practice Example

According to the intake sheet, Angela sought counseling for "marital problems. I'm not happy with things the way they are." She had a lot of reasons not to be happy. Her husband of 12 years was a difficult man. He was moody, and more often than not, the mood was dark, depressed, and negative. He had trouble controlling his anger and was apt to get mad, puff up, and walk out at the slightest provocation. Often, Angela had no idea what she said or did to make him angry.

He was equally volatile with their two girls, ages 5 and 7. One minute, he would be playing with them in the living room, and the next, he would yell at them to settle down and be quiet so he could read the paper. Consequently, the girls never knew what he wanted from them. Over time, they avoided interacting with him. Angela felt sure that his unpredictable moods were the reason behind her older daughter's bedwetting.

The husband also demanded sex constantly. If he was home, Angela never felt free to sit down and read a book or watch TV. The minute she wasn't moving, he approached her for sex. He whispered in her ear, touched her, made lewd remarks, and so on. He had also been nagging her for years to allow a third party into their sexual encounters. Although she was resolutely against the idea, he continued to bring it up.

After several months of therapy, Angela was certain that she should leave the marriage. She had no positive feelings left for her husband, and it was becoming clear that his demanding and unhappy demeanor was affecting the children.

When she intimated to him that divorce was an option she was considering, he fell apart and told her he would do anything it took to save the marriage. She felt sorry for him and agreed to work toward reconciliation. They began marital therapy, but he was resistant to the therapist's suggestions, and his behavior basically did not change. The marital therapy ended when he stormed out of session in a rage one day.

Angela had financial support from her family, as well as the emotional support of her friends and extended family, and although her older daughter's therapist agreed that a conflicted relationship with the father was behind the bed-wetting, she still could not make a move to get out of the marriage. Her Minnesota Multiphasic Personality Inventory (MMPI) indicated that she was experiencing strong feelings of helplessness and vulnerability.

Finally, following yet another episode when her husband pressured her for sex, Angela told him no and meant it. Five months later, they were still not having sex, and she was still unable to file for divorce. It was time for the Rock-Hard Resolve technique.

Angela took a long time picking over the rocks to find the right one. She chose a small, flat, black one. "I'm drawn to this one," she said. "It fits my hand." The rock was a symbol of the resolve and strength she discovered when she told her husband to stay away from her and not bother her for sex. She kept the rock on the dashboard of her car. Every time she ran an errand, transported a child, or drove to an appointment, she looked at her rock and was reminded of her strength. Several weeks later, she saw an attorney and filed for divorce.

Of course, the rock technique was not *the* reason that Angela was able to move on, but it was a nice part of helping her find her own resolve and sense of self—something she had lost in her marriage.

A Matter of Perspective

When I discussed this tool in my book *Group Exercises for Adolescents: A Manual for Therapists*, I noted that the technique was equally valuable for use in individual therapy. It's true. I can't say that it is something you'll want to keep on top of your toolbox, but you will be glad you have it with you for a few special projects.

There are those clients who can be helped a great deal if only their perspective were different. From their vantage point, the focus is so narrow that they have lost sight of other possibilities. They may be mired in the mud of a mind-set from which they cannot extricate themselves. Like quicksand, the struggle causes them to only sink deeper into the muck. If we can help them develop a different perspective, we have been of service for sure.

Instructions

There are times when you might want to talk to your client directly about perspective, and times when actions speak louder than words. If you want to use the more logical, rational, linear approach, remind your client that perspective is everything. Go ahead and use the visual aid of a half-full glass of water if you think it will help. Present your client with the glass, and ask if it is half-full or half-empty. Play devil's advocate, and whatever perspective he or she chooses, you choose the opposite. The point will be made. Then, you can offer other ways to see the situation in question.

If drama and surprise would better make the point, let your client experience the transformation that a changed perspective offers. Simply lie down on the floor and put your legs in your chair. (Place your butt near the base of your chair and your lower legs on the chair seat. This anatomically correct posture will not strain the back.) Invite your client to join you. So, there you both are, upside down, facing the ceiling. Nothing seems the same. The whole office looks and feels different, although it is exactly as it was before you changed positions. A picture is worth a thousand words!

You can go right ahead and continue your conversation for a while; the physical shift may open up your client to more than one new awareness and a greater degree of comfort expressing him- or herself.

Practice Example

Stacy and Jerry had been having an affair. Stacy, age 44, was divorced, and Jerry, age 53, was married. Their dangerous liaison had been going on for 13 years. Jerry was a supervisor in a food processing plant, and Stacy was the company's personnel director.

Initially, I was seeing Stacy. Her secret life was taking its emotional toll. She thought surely people knew, but she carried the truth alone. Not even her best girlfriends had a clue. It would be too dangerous for Jerry. Jerry was always going to leave his wife, Peg. First, he had to wait until the kids were gone. Then, he had to wait until the redecorating project in their home was finished. Then, it was that trip he had always promised his wife, the Christmas holidays, and so on. The delays were unending.

Stacy was a bright, personable woman, and I liked her a lot. Frankly, I developed a bit of a loathing for Jerry (he was "Jerry the weasel" in my thought life, I'm afraid), so when Stacy arranged a couples session, I was more a mother bird than an objective therapist at the beginning of the session. However, my preconceptions blew away like so many feathers. Jerry was a nice guy, doing the best he could with what he had at the time. What he had was a deep affection for Stacy and a load of guilt about leaving his wife, whom he valued as a good person and a great mother. Unfortunately, he had not been in love with her for years. He was in love with Stacy. His wife adored him, and although their sex life began to evaporate years ago, she accepted it as a consequence of aging. Jerry's read on her position was that sex had never been very important to her, so the loss of that marital obligation was more a relief than a mystery.

Jerry and Peg had a wide circle of friends and a close relationship with Jerry's family, all of whom lived in the area. They enjoyed a good relationship with Peg's family as well, but most of them were in Alaska, where she grew up. That was yet another thing about which Jerry felt guilty.

As I listened to this couple and watched them together, my heart ached in sympathy. Jerry actually seemed in more pain than Stacy about their plight. I wondered aloud if he might benefit from an individual session or two. He agreed that indeed he would, and we arranged an individual session.

Jerry was stymied by guilt. Divorcing his wife of 29 years meant that he had failed—as a husband, a father, a friend, a provider, a man. He could hardly tolerate the contemplation of the pain Peg would endure if he left her. She was a good person, and she deserved better. His family loved Peg and would not understand; his grown children most certainly would be upset. There was no room for divorce in his Roman Catholic roots, either.

Jerry loved Peg like a sister. The thought of anything physical with her was off-putting. He did not want to hold her, caress her, or really even touch her, and he seldom did if he could get by with it. The sight of her body was not in the least appealing. He was racked with guilt because with Stacy, it was just the opposite, and it had been for years. After all these years together as lovers, he still could hardly keep his hands off of her.

He had pleasant experiences with his wife, but his world was transformed when he and Stacy were together. They were on the same wavelength. Their sense of humor, interests, values—everything—was perfect.

My session with Jerry turned into several sessions. Jerry was thoroughly trapped in a drift of guilt that was so heavy it was crushing the life out of him. Stacy was the prize he could never win.

One day in session, I plunked myself down on the floor, used the seat of my chair to support my legs (as described in the Instructions section), and invited Jerry to join me. I challenged him to consider a different perspective. We began to talk about his right to happiness. We talked about the possibility that by staying with Peg, he was dooming her to a loveless life. Most wives do not want their husbands to love them like a sister. His frozenness prevented everyone from finding his or her heart's desire, to love and be loved by the right person. Maybe God, even the God of the Roman Catholic Church, would not want Jerry to be relegated to a life of quiet desperation. Basically, we "tried on" some other ways to look at the situation.

The session marked the beginning of a process that led to Jerry and Peg divorcing. Peg was sad, but she did not die of a broken heart. The kids were disappointed, but they did not abandon their father. Jerry found a church that held a less condemning perspective on divorce. Stacy and Jerry began to date in public. They were having a blast!

It's what keeps us in the business . . . happy endings now and then.

Suggested Reading

Carrell, S. (1999). *Group exercises for adolescents: A manual for therapists.* Thousand Oaks, CA: Sage.

Bridging the Gap
Getting Beyond Insight

I n the course of writing *The Therapist's Toolbox*, I contacted three authors to ask if I could borrow their tools. Over the years, these ingenious ideas have become standards in my toolbox, and I would hate to work without them. My intent was to loan them out.

The process of obtaining permission (or not) was an interesting experience. I knew Paula Caplan personally (see Chapter 26, "The Mother Interview"), but the other two authors were strangers. I called Paula, and, in her predictably big-hearted way, she gave me permission to use her material without hesitation. Then, I sent a letter to the publishing company of one of the other authors. In a timely manner, a representative of the publishing house responded by mail. No, I most certainly could not use anything from the book was the reply. Then, I managed to contact the other author, Susan Campbell, by e-mail. Ms. Campbell responded immediately, giving me permission to use the particular idea I wanted from one of her books (see Chapter 12, "The Paper Exercise"). She also suggested that I might find another tool or two from a newer book, *From Chaos to Confidence* (see "Suggested Reading" at the end of this exercise). I was intrigued with her generosity and openness and wanted to know more, so I ordered the book.

Her book explains her generous and open response to my query. In a very real way, it's what the book is all about. Basically, she says that there are two ways to respond to change or transition or the unknown: the "Security/Control" mind-set, and the "Learning/Discovery" mind-set. People locked in the Security/Control mode react to change or transition

---

NOTE: The exercise described in this chapter is adapted from Susan Campbell, *From Chaos to Confidence: Survival Strategies for the New Workplace*, New York: Simon & Schuster. Copyright © 1996 by Susan Campbell. Used by permission.

or the unknown with attempts to gain or maintain control. Loss of control means loss of security to this way of thinking; therefore, the need to be in control of situations and people is very high.

The Learning/Discovery perspective is quite different. Change is seen as an opportunity for learning new things and for personal growth. In her book, Ms. Campbell makes a good argument for the success of the Learning/Discovery reaction to change over the Security/Control reaction.

In my work as a chaplain, I talk about a mentality of Scarcity versus a mentality of Abundance. I think it is related. People who operate out of a mind-set of scarcity believe that there is not enough for everybody; therefore, they had better get in there and get theirs. Once they get theirs, they must be vigilant about protecting it. Those who operate out of a perspective of abundance believe that God (or the Force, or Fate) provides plenty for everyone; therefore, letting go and sharing are the order of the day. I imagine that the publishing house of the other author operates out of the Security/Control and Scarcity mind-sets. Therefore, I was not allowed to promote their book, as I would have liked.

On the other hand, I could not recommend Susan Campbell's book, *From Chaos to Confidence*, more highly. It is written for the workplace, and her focus is on developing more successful ways to cope with the ever-changing nature of the workplace these days. She does an excellent job explaining her theory for the workplace, but it has a much broader message. When I read it, I was working with a client who was trying to get the courage to get out of an unsatisfying, unhappy marriage. She had been in therapy for about a year, and she had all of the insight known to men, women, and God about why she needed to leave and why it was hard for her to do so. But she was stalled, immobile, frozen, unable or unwilling to make a move toward getting out. How often do we see this? If you are like me, all the time! Sometimes, gaining insight does *not* take one halfway there; sometimes, it's only a fraction of the distance toward meaningful change.

I used this exercise, which is new to me and comes from Susan's book. It was just the tool for my stuck client. The technique enabled her to not only identify the roadblocks along her path to freedom, but also conceptualize ways to maneuver around them. I think it's a winner! It's nice to get a new tool for your box now and then.

Instructions

This is one of those tools that, depending on the situation, you may want to use right in your office during session or send home with your clients. I prefer assigning it as homework.

Tell your client that you would like him or her to represent on paper the dilemma you are working on together. Invite him or her to draw something that represents where he or she is right now in one corner of the paper. This should be a symbolic drawing that depicts the current state of things. Then, at the opposite corner, draw (symbolically) the desired outcome. Finally, identify and illustrate each and every roadblock or obstacle perceived that must be overcome in order to reach the desired state or goal.

Second, suggest that your client include all of the support mechanisms that will help him or her negotiate the roadblocks successfully. The second part can be done simultaneously with the roadblocks, or assigned as a separate project for a later session. You will know which is the better assignment for your client.

Finally, process the drawing with your client at your next session.

Practice Example

Pam came to therapy because of "relationship difficulties." She and Barry had been together for 5 years. They met during their sophomore year in college, and they moved in together after dating for several months. Pam graduated in 4 years, but Barry did not. He had changed majors several times and lacked certain courses to complete the major he had most recently chosen, art and design. Not finishing things in a timely manner was Barry's signature. He had trouble ending relationships (he and his old girlfriend still talked on the phone) and trouble managing his finances (he was apt to spend money he didn't have eating out, going to movies, attending concerts, or buying expensive books). Pam finally took over the financial management of the apartment because Barry would let the phone, rent, or utility bills go unpaid. Not long ago, their cable service had been cut off because Barry had not paid the bill when it was his turn.

Pam was in her second job since graduating from college. Initially, she worked in the Chamber of Commerce. After about a year, she applied for a higher-paying and more prestigious position in the alumni office of a local university. Barry languished in his career, working as a florist while he took courses to complete his degree. Progress in school was slow because he could take only a course or two at a time with his work schedule and tuition costs; however, he had recently lost an entire semester because he couldn't seem to make it to the early morning class.

Pam loved Barry's free spirit and spontaneity. She appreciated his intelligence and sense of humor, but his irresponsible behavior was taking its toll on her affection. Things came to a head 2 months earlier when Pam became ill with a colon disease. She was in the hospital for 5 days, and Barry was much less than an attentive, concerned partner. When one of his buddies called with the proposition of a "road trip" to a nearby city, "just for a blow-out weekend," Barry agreed to go, leaving Pam in the hospital. When he returned, she met him with every intention of breaking up. Barry wept and begged and promised and swore undying love, and Pam took him back. It was the fifth time she had done so.

Since then, it had just been more of the same. He was not doing well in his art history class, and his supervisor at work threatened to fire him if he couldn't get to work on time. His car needed repairs, but he spent all of his extra money on new skis.

Pam had been wildly passionate about Barry at first. His looks and physique appealed to her, as did his artistic perspective on life, but at this point, she avoided having sex with him. He was such a child! She was not interested in being sexual with a little boy.

Pam knew she needed to terminate the relationship but had lost all faith in her ability to do so. She thought therapy might help.

I assigned the gap exercise as homework and sent Pam off with several large sheets of paper and a box of markers. The next week, when she came in for her appointment, she rolled the paper out on the floor of my office and we processed her work.

At the lower corner was a drawing of the head of a sad-looking woman (Pam) inside a cage (a square box with bars across the face). The picture represented where she was now. She felt trapped in her relationship with Barry. The cage was her guilt about pulling out of the relationship. At the opposite upper corner, was a blue sky with puffy white clouds, a bright yellow sun, and a brightly colored kite on a string. This picture represented where she wanted to be, free and flying high. Between the two pictures, was a diagonal line with stepping stones on one side of the line, and stumbling blocks on the other side. One of the stumbling blocks was a single stick figure inside a circle colored black. This drawing represented Pam's fear of being alone. She said that before doing the exercise, she had not realized that one of the things that kept her in the cage was her own fear. Another stumbling block was the figure of an angel, complete with halo and wings. This represented her need to feel like she was a good person, that she could overlook her own needs and desires in the care and service of others.

Directly across from the angel figure, on the stepping-stone side of the line, was an inverted "V" with a line across it. On either end of the line was a circle with "25 lbs." written inside. This stepping-stone concept allowed her to move forward in spite of the angel stumbling block. "This symbolizes the balance that I should have in this relationship," she said.

"See, I think it's out of balance; Barry's not giving me very much. I'm doing almost all of the work."

Another stepping stone was a floating dollar bill. Pam would be able to manage her financial obligations and assets better without Barry in her life. She had also drawn a cell phone and a pen and paper on the stepping-stone side of the line. She said it symbolized that writing him a letter or phoning him instead of confronting him directly could help manage the fear she had of breaking up with him face-to-face.

A sad face with tears streaming down (Barry's face) stood for her fear of his pain. She could not think of a way to get past that, so I noted a direction to go in our future work together—namely, a focus on boundary issues and conversation about her need to save or rescue others.

There was a valentine heart with an arrow through it inside the universal symbol for "No!" (a circle with a diagonal line through it). She did not want to be back out in the singles scene again, trying to find someone to date. She hated that worse than anything. On the other hand, across from that, was a stick figure family, a mom and dad and two children. The family represented her desire to find a life partner and eventually have a family.

Clearly, the exercise helped Pam document, organize, and explore the journey she would make to secure the freedom she desired. It also generated a number of areas on which to work in future sessions.

Suggested Reading

Campbell, S. (1996). *From chaos to confidence: Survival strategies for the new workplace.* New York: Simon & Schuster.

Field Trips

Sometimes, for therapists, "thinking outside the box" means thinking outside the office. It's hard to broaden your horizons when everything you learned in shrink school about doing therapy was about doing it in the context of an office.

I first experimented with a field trip because I was having difficulty trying to help a client who was a survivor of sexual abuse. The experiment worked so well that I took two more trips with clients who, likewise, were haunted by experiences from childhood and adolescence. Finally, a client invited me on a field trip with her. Now, although taking a field trip is not something I do very often, it is in my toolbox, and if I need it, I know how to use it.

I hope that these trip ideas will be useful as examples and may even become catalysts to spark your own creative wanderings.

Trip #1: Recovering Reality

I know people who can tell you where they sat in their second-grade classroom and what they took for lunch. I can't even remember the second grade! The point is that the ability to retain childhood memories varies greatly among individuals for a variety of reasons. I think my second-grade memories are remote because I was safe and protected and happy then. There were no traumas, no profound learnings, and no noteworthy joyous events for me in the second grade, so I didn't make any entries in my logbook.

I think most of us lose touch with how we were; how we acted; how we looked; and what it was like to be 4, 5, 7, or 9 years old. If you are working with a client who was traumatized at a certain age, and you think it would be therapeutic, consider recapturing reality by becoming observers of children the same age. You might want to make arrangements with a school, church, or other institution where children could be observed without interfering with their schedule or activities. Also, consider public places where children gather as a destination for your field trip. This might be a public park, playground, skating rink, or baseball field. Sometimes, I meet my client at my office and drive him or her to our destination; other times, we meet at the appointed place. Given the legal/ethical implications of transporting a client in your car, it is safer to meet at the destination, but if I have therapeutic reasons for accompanying my client, I don't always play it safe.

If you are going to a school classroom or another setting where conversation with your client during observation would be disruptive, take notepads and paper for both of you. Record observations, impressions, and questions about the experience. You will have an agenda for your next session. Sometimes, you will need to process the event immediately. If you anticipate that, schedule 2 hours or more for your field trip. If you decide to review the experience in your next session, ask your client to bring his or her notes (if notes were taken) or write about the experience (if notes were not taken).

Practice Example

I had been working with a woman who was sexually abused by her stepfather from age 5 through age 12. Her treatment involved dealing not only with the horror of the abuse and how terrorized she was by it, but also with the abandonment she felt when, at age 12, she started getting her period and her stepfather never touched her again. It was a complicated case.

After 3 years of therapy, she still struggled with a number of issues. One was the belief that somehow, she could have and should have done something to stop the abuse. I had done everything I knew to do to help her see the fallacy of this belief, but to no avail.

Then, I had an idea. A friend of mine was the director of a local preschool. I phoned her to see if it might be possible to visit her school one day. I explained that I would like to bring someone with me. I told her it would be helpful to this person to be able to observe children around the age of 5 or 6. I'm sure she guessed I was talking about a client, although I did not say that, of course. She would be delighted to have us visit, she said. Actually, her school was set up for observation so that parents of prospective students could see the operation in progress during school hours, and so parents of enrolled students could watch their children for a variety of reasons.

When we arrived at the school, we were directed to the observation deck, which overlooked the open classrooms. The assistant pointed out the classroom for 5- and 6-year-olds. We observed the children for about 40 minutes.

The impact of watching these little ones was profound for my client. Their innocence, vulnerability, openness, curiosity, and dependence on the adults caring for them was obvious. She could see that 5- or 6-year-old children had little to no power over anything, even themselves. The experience enabled her to change her false belief that she could have stopped the abuse by her stepfather.

This experience did not mark the end of more struggles or more therapy for my client, but it was an important step toward recovery.

Trip #2: The Importance of Place

Sometimes, the location of a traumatic event holds the key to recovery. If you discern that your client associates a traumatic episode with a particular place, consider going there with your client—returning to the scene of the crime, so to speak. This may not be possible if the event occurred in a distant place, but if it did not, take your client on a field trip. It may be that a corrective emotional experience can be created if the locale of the original trauma is revisited.

If it is impossible for you to revisit the site, could your client do so without you? This may not be ideal, but with proper preparation and other supportive individuals along (if necessary), a positive outcome is possible. If returning to the scene is not practical, consider revisiting the place through guided imagery.

Practice Examples

Greg came to therapy because his sponsor in Alcoholics Anonymous (AA) recommended it. Greg had been through inpatient treatment for his alcoholism more than once. He tended to do well for a year or so after treatment, but would relapse shortly after his 1-year anniversary of sobriety in AA. The last time he relapsed, he lost almost everything—his second wife, his relationship with his children, and his oldest friend, who had always been there for him. The only thing that survived was his job as personnel director of a manufacturing plant, and he was hanging on to it by a thread.

His AA sponsor told Greg that his self-esteem was so damaged that the sponsor did not know how to help him. Individual therapy with a professional seemed the most logical direction.

I do not work with substance abuse clients per se, but I agreed to see Greg because he had treatment experience and a solid connection to the AA community.

As we unwrapped the bandages that covered the wounds in his life, we exposed an open lesion. His 2 years of junior high school had been grisly. He was always on the fringes of the popular group, but never allowed in. The harder he tried to win the approval of his peers, the more distant they became. He changed his identity like so many clothes. He tried being a jock, but he could not pull it off because he was small and not well coordinated. He tried being the "prep" and ran for student offices, but was never elected. Then, he became a rebel in an attempt to win attention and respect from his peers, but that only made matters worse. Now, the teachers and administration seemed to join with his peers in the critical, rejecting atmosphere he felt at school. By October of his eighth-grade year, he was miserable. School became a personification of rejection. Although he had a few boys he considered friends, he continued to long for inclusion in groups that did not welcome him. He hated the sight of the school and the smell in the hallways. The gymnasium symbolized failure; he could not excel in athletics, and he felt out of place and alone in the assemblies that were held there.

The emotional pain was obvious in Greg's face as he recounted first one story, then another. These experiences might as well have happened last week instead of 29 years ago. He had carried a perception of himself as an unlovable failure into his adult life. Positive experiences and accomplishments of adulthood had not changed the dark image that resided below the surface of his consciousness.

I suggested that we pay a visit to his junior high school. Uncertainly, he agreed to try it. It was summer, and classes were not in session. The small parking lot and grounds surrounding the school were deserted. We walked all the way around the old red brick building in silence. We climbed the steps to the front doors and peeked in through the windows. We sat on the brick walls of the stoop. I encouraged Greg to take another tour around the building, alone. I told him that he could do anything—cry or yell or curse . . . whatever he needed to do to express his feelings. I would stay on the stoop and wait for him. In a few minutes, I could hear him yelling, and could hear rocks hitting the old brick walls. "You son of a bitch!" he yelled. "You don't own me anymore! You're a powerless, aging old fart!"

He returned in a few minutes, and we talked about his perceptions. The school was so much smaller than he remembered, so much less daunting than the image that resided in his memory. He shook his head and laughed; he was a little embarrassed, I think. How could he have allowed this childhood experience to color his whole life?

It would have been nice if he could have walked the halls and looked into that gymnasium, but it was summer, and the school was closed, so we did what we could. I believe that my presence was important; I bore witness to the exorcism of a haunting memory.

Tom was a recently divorced 51-year-old attorney. He had been married for 27 years when his wife told him she wanted out. Although the marriage was lackluster, Tom accepted things as they were. He had a busy practice, had his children (now in college) whom he loved, had a lovely home in the country, and had his golf buddies. Tom had long believed that being successful was the path to the good life, so he was dumbstruck when his wife told him she was not willing to live like this anymore and wanted a divorce. The sudden turn of events left Tom feeling like a failure, and like a stranger in his own life. Through the encouragement of his law partner, who had gone through a difficult divorce himself, Tom entered therapy in an attempt to make sense of things.

Looking back, Tom began to see that his focus on the external, material manifestations of life had blurred his vision. He had been blind to the internal dimensions of success and began to see that the key to happiness might be hidden in a different place.

His wife had told him in many ways, for many years, that her needs were not being met. He had minimized her complaints, thinking that most women seemed vaguely dissatisfied with their lot but got over it. He began to understand that his lack of response to her was not only an attempt to avoid conflict, but also a passive-aggressive move that kept him in control. Over time, he was able to acknowledge a profound fear of criticism. As long as he appeared strong, adequate, and in control, he was safe from facing his own fears of inadequacy.

Therapy with Tom was like a mining expedition. We would peer into a crack of his consciousness, shine a light into the dark places, and dig for the vein of fear that might become a valuable resource. In the process, we discovered the mother lode and unearthed a few surprises as well.

Among the surprises was Tom's fear of heights. Although this was not a fear that defined or controlled his life, as others did, when it came out in therapy, it was clear that conquering, or at least making peace with, this old enemy was important to him. He recounted the times that this monster reared its head. Sometimes, it happened when he went skiing, which he did every winter. If he approached the crest of a rise that he couldn't see over, he panicked. Occasionally, it happened when he was driving in the hilly countryside. If he crested a hill and couldn't see over it, panic set in. On a vacation in Colorado with his family one year, he drove from Estes Park to Winter Park, across Trail Ridge Drive. This drive is famous for spectacular mountain views and sheer drops for hundreds of feet from the side of the road. It was almost more than Tom could handle. Although his wife could see that something was wrong and offered to drive, he would not hear of it. Finally, sweating and shaking, he arrived at their destination. Feeling weak and ashamed of his overwhelming fear, he could not speak the truth. Instead, he told his family that he must have the flu and begged off going to dinner that night.

He knew the pattern; when visibility over the edge of a precipice was compromised, he panicked. *Panic* was the correct word. Shortness of breath, nausea, a sense of impending doom, perspiration, and light-headedness characterized these occasions. He knew it when the symptoms came, but he did not know what started the syndrome in the first place.

Then, one day, it all came back to him. He had gone to his mother's house to see about her garage door opener. First, the garage door responded to the remote inconsistently, and now it was failing to respond at all. His mother lived in the house in which he had grown up, an old bungalow in a midtown neighborhood. The large front porches, mature landscaping, and detached garages created a nostalgia that now was attracting young couples to the area.

As Tom approached the garage, he eyed its roof, wondering if it was time to think about a new one. Suddenly, a memory flashed in his mind's eye. It was summer, and he was up on the garage roof with his father and his uncle. The two men were putting on a new roof, and he had begged to join them. He was only 7 or 8, too young for such a venture, but he had begged, and the men had obliged. Now he was in over his head. The roof had not seemed threatening from his vantage point on the ground, but everything looked different once he climbed the ladder. When he turned and looked down, he could not see over the roof's edge. The height of the building upon which he stood seemed unfathomable to the young boy. He thought he was going to die, and there was no one to call for help. His father and uncle, working close by, laughed at him, and he was embarrassed.

Just remembering the event elicited symptoms of panic. Tom stood in his mother's driveway, panting and feeling nauseated. He recounted the incident in his next therapy session, and we decided that a field trip was in order.

The next week, we returned to the scene together. Tom got a ladder from the garage and climbed to the roof as I watched from below. Once on the rooftop, he turned and looked down. Then, he laughed. "Good God!" he said with a snort, "I could jump from here and not even get hurt!" The source of his fantastic terror was diminished to reality by taking a field trip with his therapist.

Although this event was just a detour on Tom's search for self-understanding, it was well worth the trip.

Trip #3: A Comfortable Spot

There may be times when inviting your client to a session in the park (or at the zoo, or by the lake, etc.) might have therapeutic consequences. Some people are more at ease outside the therapist's office. Experiencing the beauty of a natural setting together could enhance the relationship. It may never be a usual method for you, but once in a while, it could be just what a client needs.

Practice Example

Betty had been my client for more than 4 years. She was a high-functioning borderline personality disorder (BPD) with comorbid diagnoses of post-traumatic stress disorder and major depression. She had a history of hospitalization for suicidal ideation and parasuicidal acting out.

Betty was a businesswoman who owned and managed her own business, a successful beauty shop that supported five hair stylists, two nail technicians, and a massage therapist. The staff rented space from Betty and paid her a percentage of their income. The nature of the business created complicated relationships with indistinct boundaries between employer, employee, and client. Boundary issues were difficult for Betty.

Initially, in my work with her, we had our own boundary struggles. She called between sessions more than any other client I've ever had. Of course, this behavior is common in individuals with BPD, and always a challenge. Usually, I do not have hard-and-fast rules about calls between sessions with my client population because it is not necessary. My clients seldom phone unless it is to confirm an appointment time or cancel an appointment. There are exceptions to this rule, and Betty was one. After numerous calls, I addressed this in session one day and explained that between-session phone calls were against office policy unless it was a crisis situation. Shortly after that, Betty began calling again, always in a "crisis" situation. The crisis involved hints of suicidal acting out. Statements such as, "I'm so confused and overwhelmed, I just can't take it anymore" or "I hate my life . . . it's just not worth the effort!" were common.

Sometimes, the calls got lengthy. Finally, I instituted another boundary; when calls went longer than 15 minutes, I started charging. She continued to call, ending the conversation right at the 15-minute cutoff.

Betty was an amazing woman. She was the survivor of childhood sexual abuse by her older brother and his friends. The abuse went on for years. Her first husband wasn't much different. But in spite of the horrors of her past, she was intelligent, interesting, and very funny. I really liked her and respected her resourcefulness. I felt her between-session phone calls were necessary in our relationship, like learning the steps before we could dance.

I almost blew it, however, when she asked one day if I would be willing to spend our session walking at a nature park not far from the office. My knee-jerk response was to think, "Oh brother! Here we go again, pushing the limits!" She told me she just knew she would be more relaxed outside of my office. Being outdoors would remove the feeling of being in a clinical setting, which she hated.

We had spent many sessions struggling with her resistance to therapy. That is, she would use most of the session talking to me about how much she did not want to talk to me. Although this was frustrating, I kept telling myself that it was a necessary part of the process and hung in there. But this request to leave the office and take a walk with her so she could "talk to me better" was going too far! Just how special did this woman need to feel?, I asked myself. I was very close to drawing a line in the sand when it occurred to me that I was about to execute a power move without enough information. She really was not asking all that much, I reasoned, so I decided to go with it and see what happened.

Well, nothing much happened, and everything happened. Just as she had predicted, she was much more comfortable in the outdoor setting than she had ever been in the office. She was more talkative, relaxed, and open. It was a productive session, and our relationship became more trusting after that. Partly, I was willing to accommodate her in this, and partly, she was simply telling the truth.

Because the field trip worked so well with her, I occasionally take walks with other clients. Betty was a good teacher.

Rituals and Other Blessings

The threads of ritual woven into the fabric of a society may determine its strength. Unfortunately, in our culture, important remnants of civilization were swept away in the backwash as the tide of the post-modern era inched its way forward. Technological advance captured the imagination of most, and time-honored customs and traditions were tossed away. We are beginning to know better.

Thanks to media technology, the work of scholars such as Joseph Campbell has elevated the consciousness of the general public. The enlightened and informed are taking another look at ancient maps as they search for health and happiness. At least some of the routes to what we seek are right under our noses. The rediscovery of ritual as an important element in life is buried treasure indeed. As therapists, we have the opportunity to offer the healing possibilities to our clients. The place to start is with us.

If I were to take "The Ritual Test for Health and Happiness," I might not do too poorly. My husband and I have our rituals. We have one for parting company when one of us leaves the house, called the "H&K" (hug and kiss). We have our Friday-night ritual: We don't go out, and we don't have people in. We stay at home, do not answer the telephone, have dinner by candlelight, share a bottle of wine, and snuggle on the couch. We take a vacation at the same time every year and go to essentially the same place. When we do these little rituals, we remember who we are as a couple. It is defining.

Our family rituals are also well defined. What we do at Christmas, when we do it, and with whom is the same, year after year. All high holidays have their rhythm and flow and predictable tone.

I am blessed with a number of friends with whom I share history. I have three girlfriends from high school with whom I meet regularly. We have lunch together once a month. At Christmas, we have dinner at the country club and sit at the same table. We have been meeting in this way for 15 years. It all started at our 20th high school reunion, another ritual.

When I went off to college, I took potluck for a roommate and lucked out. Susan, whom I nicknamed Boo-Boo, became my best friend. We chummed up with some other girls down the hall. Together, we supported and encouraged each other through that first year away from home, through bad grades and boyfriends and hangovers and sorority rush. Thirty years later, the group is still in my life. The five of us live in five different states, but every 3 years, we gather for a reunion, no husbands and no kids allowed. We hole up to swap our woes, set our goals, and bare our souls. I'm sure it's why none of us has been in long-term therapy.

I meet on a regular basis with a group of women to examine our deeply held values and explore our spiritual lives. We call ourselves "Girlfriends Group," and we are spiritual friends. It all started in response to the transition imposed upon us when our children left home. Suddenly, our children were gone. We looked up at the breakfast table one day and discovered that our husbands were still there. They were older, they were fatter, they were balder, and they were still behind the newspaper. Some of us weren't sure we liked them much anymore. We agreed that intentional conversation about our collective plight would be a good thing. We signed on for an 8-week commitment; that was 6 years ago. New rituals have their place.

I belong to a church whose source of authority is Scripture, reason, and tradition. The tradition part is as important as anything else. We are a liturgical church, so the essential elements of our worship service are the same as they were when it all started. The order of service is the same everywhere. When I step into an Episcopal church anywhere on the planet, I'm home. Ritual matters.

The following are ideas for you to use with your clients. The rituals you share with them will probably not solve everything, but they will matter.

Letting-Go Rituals

Sand Tray

The sand tray is a versatile tool. When you have clients who need to have a funeral for a part of themselves that has died, or for a person in their lives who has died, or for a relationship that has died, consider using your sand tray. See Chapter 2, page 17, on creating a sand tray.

Prepare your clients for the ceremony by explaining how important rituals are. Help them understand how rituals have been a healing modality since recorded history. Ask about their own rituals, such as weddings, funerals, and high holidays. Don't forget to ask about their personal rituals: When do they brush their teeth, before or after breakfast? Could they put their pants on with the other leg first? How do they begin their day? Then, discuss having a ritual to mark this place in their lives.

Instruct your client to find symbols for what needs to be buried. If he or she is putting his or her silent acceptance of the unacceptable to rest, maybe the symbol is something that represents quiet acquiescence. A little character from your sand tray collection might work, such as a lamb or other passive creature. Perhaps a bandanna or duct tape would symbolize the gag that has been over his or her mouth for so long.

If your client is silencing a message that has defined him or her, find a way to symbolize it. You could use a rubber band for the weakness that has characterized him or her, or an angel ornament to symbolize perfection. A rock might stand for the unforgiving or judgmental nature he or she would like to let go of, or a piece of eggshell for the oversensitivity that has caused him or her so much distress.

Your client might need to bury the power that another, or others, have had over him or her. Find a way to represent that other, or others, and use it in your ritual.

Maybe someone died a long time ago. That does not mean that that person's influence is dead, or that your client has accepted his or her death. A second "funeral" in your office might be helpful.

Use all of the aids at your disposal to emphasize the ritual. Play music, use candles, or develop liturgy (a written service or ceremony follows).

Practice Example: Putting Grandfather to Rest

Fourteen-year-old Nathan was depressed. His frantic mother brought him to therapy when all of her attempts to "fix" her son had failed. She sent him to summer camp, took him and a buddy on a weekend vacation to a theme park, and enrolled him in tae kwan do lessons. She cooked his favorite meals and encouraged him to have friends spend the night. She and her boyfriend took him to the lake and taught him to water ski. Nothing really worked. He remained quiet and withdrawn and generally disinterested in everything. His mother was worried sick.

Nathan's father died of a heart attack when Nathan was nine. His beloved grandfather died 2½ years later. Nathan had seemed perfectly fine until this year. Suddenly, the light disappeared from Nathan, and darkness prevailed. The child psychiatrist agreed that young Nathan was depressed and prescribed an antidepressant. Still, a month later, apathy and lack of energy defined his days.

It did not take long to get a handle on the issue in therapy. When Nathan's father died so suddenly, his maternal grandfather stepped in. He was determined to fill the gap that Nathan's father left in his son's life. It was a wonderful opportunity for Grandpa Pat, who had three daughters; Nathan became the son he had never had. Before long, Grandpa Pat became more important to Nathan than his father had ever been. Then, his grandfather died, disappearing from Nathan's life just as suddenly as his father vanished almost 4 years earlier.

Given the time and opportunity of therapy, Nathan opened the wound in his soul. The loss of the important male role models in his life shook the foundation of his faith in a stable, predictable life. For the next few weeks, we gave a wide berth to the expression of his feelings. He talked, drew, and worked in the sand tray. We discussed his relationship with his family, his friends at school, and his teachers, and we talked about his varied activities. I taught him about the stages of loss. We explored his fears. Chief among them was the fear that he would forget his grandfather. The memory of his father was already foggy, and he could not risk allowing the same process to wipe clean the slate of his grandfather's memory. It became clear that Nathan needed to learn some ways to keep his grandfather, and find a way to let his grandfather go.

First, we focused on a way to keep the memory of his grandfather. We decided on a scrapbook. With his mother's help, Nathan gathered pictures, notes, and any mementos he could find that could be used in a scrapbook. He wrote accountings of experiences they had together; one story was about a trip to see a St. Louis Cardinals baseball game, and another was about helping his grandfather grow watermelons. When Nathan seemed satisfied with his project, I turned the focus toward helping him let go.

When I suggested that we needed to put his grandfather to rest with a special ceremony, he did not bat an eye. I explained that letting his grandfather go did not mean he would forget him. It merely meant that both Nathan and his grandfather would be free to go on in their own way. We talked about the ceremony. I instructed him to bring some small items with him that were symbolic of his grandfather, and we would bury those things in the sand. He wondered if we could use a figure or two from my collection of sand tray characters. Of course we could.

We had a funeral on his next visit. Nathan brought a feather to symbolize his grandfather's gentle nature. His mother suggested that he use a marble to represent his clarity of thought. He also had an old wristwatch to stand for all the time his grandfather spent with him. I brought a fishhook for him to use because his grandfather taught him to fish. Nathan also wanted to use a Native American figure from my sand tray collection because his grandfather, like Native Americans, was knowledgable about the land and sensitive to treating it with care.

I placed candles all around the sand tray, and we dimmed the lights. I played soft music on the CD player. We ceremoniously buried the feather, marble, fishhook, and wristwatch. Nathan heaped a mound of sand over the buried objects and placed the Native American figure on top. He thought it was a good marker for his grandfather's grave. I asked Nathan if there was anything he wanted to say to his grandfather just now. He pledged not to forget him and thanked him for being his friend.

I saw Nathan only a couple of times after that. He dropped out of therapy, as people do. I hoped it was because he was doing better. I thought he was.

Balloons, Burials, and Blazes

Other letting-go rituals can be done outside of the office. This might mean a trip out to the parking lot, or a trip to a park or other setting.

One of the best ways for your client to let go of something is to write it down. Organizing one's thoughts and committing them to paper is therapeutic in and of itself. The writer will be formulating his or her own treatment plan in the process. Goals will be stated, affect will be articulated, and new behavior (the letting-go ritual) will accompany the document.

On the day of the ceremony, ask your client to read his or her work to you. Then, shred the document, place the pieces in a small plastic bag, tie the bag to a helium-filled balloon, and release it. You could dig a hole in the ground and bury it if your client prefers, or it could be set afire. When the balloon is released, your client can watch the relinquished emotion float away. If the paper is buried in the ground, he or she will heap dirt over the paper and watch it disappear. If the paper is burned, your client will watch the smoke rise up and out of sight.

Practice Example: Burying a Traumatic Childhood

Although I think it is a good idea to be with your client for these ceremonies, occasionally, I have had clients who did their ritual without me. Such was the case with Gloria.

Gloria had been in therapy with me for 2 years, and I was not her first therapist. Over the years, she had been in and out of therapy a lot. Her husband, Jack, had been by her side through it all. Like so many of my clients, Gloria was the survivor of childhood sexual abuse. The perpetrators were two older girls at school. Sexual abuse by members of one's own gender is a double betrayal. Gloria said that the healing process was like the abuse—slow to be realized, lengthy in process, and unpredictable in occurrence. Jack tried to understand his wife's trauma and recovery in every possible way. He read the books she read, attended therapy with her when appropriate, and participated in a "secondary survivors" group for the partners of sexual abuse victims. When it became time for Gloria to bury a part of her childhood trauma, she wanted to do it with him.

She decided to put her writing in a cardboard box along with some drawings and other symbolic material. She and her husband would bury the box in their backyard, in the flowerbed along the fence.

She wrote what she needed to write about the piece of her childhood that she was ready to let go of. It had to do with her pervasive distrust of women. Her son was getting married, and Gloria wanted a good relationship with her prospective daughter-in-law. She had been having nightmares about the young woman. In the dreams, the girl was always plotting and planning to harm her son in some way.

So, she put her writing and the other material in her box and brought it to session. She read me the piece and showed me the drawings. One drawing was of a simple desk, the kind found at the front of classrooms in elementary schools, the teacher's desk. The desk was brown, and the opening was shaded in black. There was the image of a face in the blackness; only the frightened eyes and frowning mouth were visible. Gloria once hid from her tormentors under her teacher's desk after school, but it was a foiled plan. The two older girls were her baby-sitters, so the principal helped them find their lost charge.

She bought an adult magazine for men and cut out several pictures of nude women in compromising positions to symbolize the end of her own forced compromises and subservience to the wretched girls. She also found a small, inexpensive Native American dream catcher, which symbolized the end of "catching her bad dreams." From now on, they could evaporate and disappear.

One evening during the following week, Gloria and Jack had their own ceremony. Jack dug a hole, and Gloria deposited the box in it. It was early fall, so she also placed an iris bulb beside the box. Her idea was that every year, she could be thankful for the beauty that grew out of even the worst of situations.

Couples Rituals

Making Rituals Out of Nothing at All

It is important to look for the role of ritual in the life of a couple. You can do a "ritual history" right along with the history of everything else. It is not necessary to ask direct questions about ritual observances—just look for evidence of the same as you get to know them. In the course of working with a couple, if you discover that they have no rituals, you have the opportunity to help them create some.

Practice Example: Lovers and Other Strangers

This is such a common malady that it might as well be the common cold. When you see it in your office, you know exactly what it is. Curing it is another matter.

There is generalized malaise in the relationship. Energy is low. Complaints of poor communication are common. Snippy retorts and bouts of conflict occur randomly. Isolated episodes of disappointment become a chronic ache.

Marilyn and Sheila met at a state teacher's convention. Marilyn taught physical education and coached the track team at a suburban high school, and Sheila was an elementary school counselor in the same school district. Marilyn was 35 and well-established in the lesbian lifestyle. She had two children from her marriage, a 13-year-old son who lived with his father, and a 10-year-old daughter who lived with her. Sheila was 26 and had never had a serious relationship, homosexual or otherwise.

Their mutual attraction soon became a deep affection that led to a serious commitment. Eighteen months after meeting, they purchased a home together. Seven years later, there was trouble in paradise.

The women articulated the familiar complaints experienced when a relationship runs into trouble. Over the years, they grew apart, finding that they had less and less in common. The relationship was not what they thought it would be. There were episodes of jealousy and big fights about money, and their sexual relationship had all but died out. But both partners were still invested in one another and wanted the relationship to work.

It was no great task to assess their communication skills. Their conversation did not flow, it splattered and bounced and sprayed all over the place. They interrupted one another willy-nilly; complete sentences were nonexistent. Their defensiveness and guardedness became a dam that blocked any potential for comfortable movement.

I learned that there were sacrosanct topics between them, and wandering onto these hallowed grounds was met with swift retribution. Marilyn's relationship with her children and Sheila's spending habits drew so much fire that the couple went miles out of their way to avoid trespassing on the sacred subjects.

Among these symptoms of relational dysfunction was a conspicuous lack of ritual. There was nothing about their meals that was consistent. They seldom sat down together to eat. Marilyn and her daughter, Amy, would grab a bite together after Amy's swim team practice a couple of times a week. On those evenings, Sheila microwaved a frozen dinner or met friends at a restaurant. They could have had coffee together in the mornings, but they did not. Sheila hurried off to her aerobics class while Marilyn fixed something for Amy. The weekends were equally inconsistent. There was no Sunday-morning ritual, and Sheila's Saturday shopping adventures without Marilyn were a sore subject. When I questioned them about their evenings, I discovered a semiritual, but it was a coming apart instead of a knitting together. Marilyn would go up to their bedroom and watch TV, and Sheila would plant herself in front of the computer in the family room until bedtime.

After several weeks of working on communication skills, I talked to them about the importance of rituals and the lack of same in their relationship. I suggested that we try to institute a couple of rituals. They were intrigued.

Success with a first attempt was encouraging. They enjoyed the Sunday-morning arrangement that they concocted in therapy. They drank coffee and read the paper together, then went for a walk at a nature center nearby, which they both liked to do. With that link soldered into place, we went after another weak connection, their evenings of isolation. As we investigated the mechanisms of their evenings, we could see the flaws. The system continued to function because certain operations were intact. Both women were classic introverts and needed some alone time in the evening to refuel. However, there was no mechanism in place to facilitate the transition from separation back to intimacy. Therefore, they stayed stuck in their own little sanctuaries.

Another factor that contributed to the maligned system was fear. Their more personal conversations were apt to stray into forbidden territory; therefore, it was safer not to risk personal (intimate) conversations at all. In fact, no conversation was the safest bet. They were safe, but they were unhappy.

As they learned that they could have successful dialogue about deeply held values (even if they did not agree) in therapy sessions, they became less fearful about trying intimate conversations at home. They decided to be intentional about having evening meals together and worked out a plan. Three times a week, they would have dinner together at home. After dinner, they would retire to their separate quarters to relax and refuel. Marilyn would watch an hour of TV, and Sheila would spend an hour on the computer. When the hour was over, they would meet on the sofa in the family room for conversation.

Integrating these simple rituals into their relationship provided opportunities for intimacy to grow. As therapists, we can do no more than provide opportunities for growth. The process of growing resides in our clients.

Religious Rituals

Practicing the Presence of God in Session

Sometimes, new clients say that they came to see me because they had heard that I was a religious person. Other times, I'll learn of a client's belief system as our work together unfolds. If you determine that your client is religious, you might honor his or her faith by simply lighting a candle at the beginning of your session to symbolize the presence of God, the Force, the Great Spirit, or whatever his or her concept of the divine might be.

I usually offer this small observance as an option. Clients who are religious appreciate the gesture. Be sure to light the candle as the session begins, in your client's presence (rather than before he or she arrives). Better yet, invite your client to do it.

An Attitude of Gratitude

This is a simple but effective ritual for your clients to institute between sessions. Suggest that they begin a gratitude list. If they are religious, they can thank the God of their understanding. If they are not religious, they can thank fate or the cosmos. Every day, they should write down at least one thing for which they are thankful. That's it! Ask them to bring their list to share with you each week for a while. The little ritual might just become a habit!

Commitment Ceremonies

As long as gay and lesbian couples cannot legally marry or receive sanction from their faith community for their union, therapists might be called upon to preside at commitment ceremonies. I know I have. I have created celebrations of commitment for clients that have taken place both in and out of my office.

Developing a service is not difficult; there are plenty of resources from which to choose. Books of prayers and poetry are helpful. Ritualize your ceremony as much as possible by using flowers, candles, and music.

If you are a licensed therapist and not an ordained priest, pastor, minister, or rabbi, there is no duality of relationship as far as I can see. You are simply responding to the felt needs of your clients, which are emotional, psychological, and spiritual.

The Mother Interview

The relationship one has with one's parents is a huge therapy issue. Certainly, there are theoretical differences about how important that relationship is, how much time should be devoted to exploring it, and how problems might best be addressed. The psychodynamic theorists, like anthropologists, devote their time and energy to digging up the ruins of the parent-child relationship. Discoveries are carefully preserved, studied, and labeled. History is everything. The behavior theorists, more like football coaches, are concerned about which skills were learned in early training and how valuable they are on the playing field today. Good techniques are encouraged, and not-so-helpful habits are extinguished. How the game is played today is what matters the most. I think most of us see value in both therapeutic approaches and develop a mix of the two that works best for us.

This tool was created with material from both theories; therefore, it is stronger than is either one when used alone. It comes from the work of Paula J. Caplan and appears in her book *Don't Blame Mother*. I have been using it for years, and it works today as well as it ever did.

Instructions

Although all children have their share of issues with a parent or parents, I see so few men who are addressing it as a therapy issue, and so many women who are, that I will be speaking of women in this section. The father/son relationship is just as complex and problem-ridden as the mother/daughter relationship, and relationships with parents of the other gender can be equally complicated. This interview can be modified

---

NOTE: Material from *Don't Blame Mother* is copyright 2000 and is reproduced by permission of Routledge, Inc., part of the Taylor and Francis Group.

to fit any parent/child combination, but I will use the mother/daughter relationship as the illustration here.

When you have a client who expresses angst about her relationship with her mother, the Mother Interview may be just the thing. My clients have used the tool successfully in a variety of situations: mothers who were preoccupied and daughters who were rebellious, daughters who were sexually abused and mothers who did not intervene, critical mothers and insecure daughters, overindulgent mothers and ungrateful daughters, controlling mothers and compliant daughters, overachieving mothers and underachieving daughters, and so on.

Help your client (the daughter) say all that she needs to say about her mother. Help her express her feelings in nonverbal ways as well. Use the Sand Tray tool, the Family Memories tool, one of the Rock tools, the Life Line tool, and the "They Didn't Mean To" tool if necessary; use whatever you can to work with the elements of the relationship in session. Then, introduce the Mother Interview.

The majority of my clients are scared to death at the notion of interviewing their mothers. The fear is that their mothers will think the interview is some tool to use against them. Basically, they are afraid that their mothers will feel blamed for something. Quite the opposite is true. The interview is meant to be both a learning process and a bonding experience.

I suggest (to those clients who are apprehensive) that they tell their mothers the interview is a therapy assignment. Their therapist, knowing how important the relationship with their mothers is, would like more information.

I go over the interview with clients in session (see Figure 26.1) and modify questions if necessary. If my client is not comfortable asking her mother a question, we simply cross that one off. When she feels comfortable with all of the questions she plans to ask, I send her out to do the interview. We will talk about the experience when she has completed it.

Practice Example

Joyce had been in therapy with me for 3 years when she did the Mother Interview. Problems with her mother did not propel her into therapy; problems with a man did.

Joyce, a 42-year-old divorced mother, was rearing her two children single-handedly. Her ex-husband was a deadbeat dad who seldom saw his children and seldom paid child support. His parents were the saving grace. They were good, hard-working people who had done well in the hardware business. They valued their former daughter-in-law and loved

1. While you were raising your children, what did you think that being a good mother meant? What did you think a good mother should do?

2. What was hardest for you about being a mother? What was your worst fear?

3. Did the experts ever give you information that went against what you thought or felt was right? Did you ever get different information from different experts?

4. Did you think that mothering should come naturally to you? If so, how did that belief affect you?

5. As a new mother, how did you feel (both positive and negative factors)? (If she doesn't raise these issues, inquire about whether she had feelings of isolation, fatigue, loss of freedom, fear, need for help of various kinds, or concerns about her identity or about the interruption of her ability to carry out her dreams or ambitions. Also ask about whether she felt love, closeness, delight, or fascination with her children.)

6. Did you want your daughter (me) to be like you? Why or why not? If yes, in what ways? If not, in what ways did you most want her to be different from you?

7. How do you feel now when you look at your daughter and notice that, in some way, she is like you?

8. How do you feel now when you look at your daughter and notice that she is different from you in some way?

9. Is it hard for you to support your daughter when she needs support that you never got or when she has opportunities that you never had? How does that feel?

10. How do you feel when your daughter does something untraditional or unusual?

11. Did you ever feel that your daughter betrayed you or let you down?

12. When have you most felt estranged from your daughter (or even felt that you had lost her)? Did that change? If so, how and why?

13. What are the pros and cons of having your daughter ask you for your advice or want your approval?

14. (If she is or was married) Have your husband and daughter ever seemed to take sides against you? Have they ever made you feel left out or inadequate or inferior?

15. What values or lessons do you hope you have imparted to your daughter?

Figure 26.1. The Mother Interview

their grandchildren. The grandparents more than made up for the child-support payments that their errant son avoided.

Joyce had been in a chaotic relationship with Chuck for 5 years. He might as well have been another child. He was irresponsible, impulsive, demanding, and self-focused. However, he was also extremely attractive, smart, and funny, and he had inherited plenty of money from his grandfather. The chemistry between them was explosive. Feeling seriously crazed, she sought therapy to help her figure out "what to do about Chuck."

As therapy progressed and she began to recover from a number of things, she wondered how she had managed to put up with someone for so long when he gave her so little. She got rid of Chuck and remained in therapy.

Joyce and her mother had always been like oil and water. She was a defiant child and rebellious adolescent, every bit as "bad" as her older sister was "good." When she refused to go to college and chose cosmetology school instead, it was the final straw. Things improved when she married a boy from her high school class and became a new mother. But when their marriage began to unravel after the birth of their second child, Joyce's mother was anything but supportive. She was appalled that Joyce would consider leaving a perfectly good man who had a good job and was not a drinker or a womanizer. The fact that Joyce was unsatisfied, unfulfilled, and unwilling to settle for a compromised life was "ridiculous" to her mother. The bridge that crossed the gap between them collapsed.

Their relationship had been strained ever since. Joyce and her husband had moved from their hometown when they married, and Joyce decided not to move back after the divorce. Being in the same town with her mother again would just be too much.

Every time Joyce called on her mother because she needed help with the children, she risked hearing that "I told you so" tone in her mother's response. When she and the children visited her parents for the weekend, her mother was forever coaching her on how she should be disciplining the children. When she came to Joyce's town to see the house Joyce had purchased, it wasn't right either. Her mother spent all her time there finding fault with the selling price, the floor plan, the condition of the bathroom fixtures, and so on. It was not pleasant. However, Joyce longed to be close to her mother. If only she could find a way to connect to her without being wounded in the process.

Joyce was making a trip to her mother's for the weekend. I thought it might be time for the Mother Interview. Initially, she was very resistant to the idea, but as we went through the questions together, she became less afraid. Yes, she thought maybe she could do it.

The interview was a turning point for the two women. The mother was surprised and honored by her daughter's interest in their relationship, and the daughter was astounded by her mother's answers. Both learned a lot about the other. They laughed and cried and shared feelings together. In the end, they discovered that they were friends.

As the two women learned to understand and validate each other's perspective, the distance between them evaporated. Finally, Joyce dared to seriously entertain the notion that her mother loved and respected her. That gave Joyce permission to love and respect herself. If she could do that, then maybe there would be no more Chuck-types in her life.

Suggested Reading

Caplan, P. J. (2000). *The new don't blame mother: Mending the mother-daughter relationship.* New York: Routledge.

Necessary Journeys

Feminist psychologists and theologians have been exploring and investigating the issues particular to women's consciousness and spirituality for a number of years. Women owe a great deal to those who have done so much work to help us understand who we are and why we do what we do. However, it's a little frustrating to see that not more women are privy to these enlightening ideas and concepts.

Women have been so identified with a patriarchal culture and point of view that we have lost a powerful connection to the feminine. I see women every day who would think, feel, and behave in more healthy ways if they only had a different framework. As therapists, we have the opportunity to present some of the more recent notions that our clients might find empowering as they face difficult situations.

For example, I talk to my clients about a genderless perspective of God if part of their struggle is with the image of God as a powerful (usually white) man with a long beard and serious frown. Sometimes, if their ideas are deeply entrenched, I use the image of a feminine God to shake them up.

A few years ago, I challenged a group of college students with whom I was working with this question: If God were a female, what would she look like? I remember their answers very well. The first young woman said, "Oh, she'd be a gypsy! She'd be tall and dark-skinned. She'd wear layers of brightly colored clothes and dance around a fire. Her long hair would fly out around her and her jewelry would jingle and clank. She would be mysterious and compelling." The next student sitting around the circle said, "She'd be big and soft and heavy breasted. She'd have on an apron and there would be smudges of flour on her face. She'd smell of bread baking." The boy next to her said, "No! She'd be a tall sexy blond in a red dress. No one could resist her. Now that's power!" The point is that these nontraditional ways of visualizing the unknown have the power to change and shape old belief patterns.

I tell my clients that as far back as recorded history, there are stories of women who are transformed by suffering. The earliest of these tales is a Sumerian poem and was recorded on stone tablets in the third millennium B.C. Other ancient cultures have stories with a similar theme. Japanese, Greek, and Roman mythology all chronicled harrowing journeys taken by goddesses. In recent history, more familiar fairy tales and myths carry this theme.

In Hans Christian Andersen's *The Little Mermaid,* a beautiful young mermaid lived an idyllic life in a kingdom under the sea. Her father was the king, and she was loved and adored by all. But one day, there was a storm on the water's surface, and a great ship capsized. A handsome young prince sank down into her underwater kingdom. She was smitten by the prince and rescued him by carrying him to shore. She could no longer live without him. The story goes on to say that the little mermaid left everything she knew—her home, the company of her family, her very essence—in order to be joined to the prince. It was a horrible and painful experience for her and, in the end, not at all what she thought it would be. She threw herself into the sea and was transformed back into a mermaid.

In the Sumerian story of Inanna, Queen of Heaven and Earth, the goddess ventured to the underworld to attend the funeral of a god. She was killed there, and her body hung on a hook to rot. Finally, her body was rescued; she was resurrected and returned home. But she returned transformed, gaining power and wisdom that she did not have before her journey.

I suggest to my clients that perhaps they are experiencing (or have experienced) some archetypal journey. Perhaps the theme of sacrifice, death, resurrection, and transformation is operative today. In order to discover their own strength and wisdom, women may need to take necessary journeys.

I have found this perspective to be both powerful and comforting for women. It suggests a way to see themselves and their situation in a more hopeful way.

Practice Example

I saw Rita only one time. She came to therapy because of the guilt that plagued her; it was like her shadow, usually invisible but following her relentlessly and then appearing when she had all but forgotten about it.

Years ago, when her children were teenagers and her husband was gone most of the time, she ran away from home. Her three boys clamored and fought and ran wild. They sabotaged whatever she did to try and keep a nice home with some degree of order. There was no money for extras in those days, she said, and no way to escape the horrible drudgery of her day-to-day existence. Her husband worked long hours as a construction worker and had no energy left at the end of his day to help her deal with the rebellious boys. He saw household chores as "women's work," so help from him in that arena had never been forthcoming. On the weekends, he mostly drank until he got drunk, yelled at the boys, and argued with her. She had been so consumed rearing the boys and managing the household that she was isolated from her women friends. Her family lived several states away. Her existence seemed a life sentence with no reprieve.

Then, one day, "I just snapped," she confessed. The boys were in school, and her husband was at work. She packed a small bag, wrote a note, and walked out the door. She moved to a nearby town, rented an apartment, and got a job. When her husband found her, he begged her to come back, but she would not. The thought of stepping back into that world of men was more than she could tolerate. She saw the boys occasionally over the next year, but most of her days and weekends were spent working or alone. She healed.

She went back home before the year was up, but everything was different. She got another job, determined never to be completely dependent on anyone again. She made household rules, and when one of the boys refused to follow them, she kicked him out. She threatened her husband with divorce if he did not do something about his drinking. His drinking behavior changed. Her life was good now, but she harbored the guilt of once abandoning her family. When anything went wrong with the boys, she blamed herself.

I talked with her about her "Necessary Journey." It was not a stretch to point out that her life was better, and that she was happier and stronger. Certainly, she was wiser. She was captivated and delighted with the concept.

Suggested Reading

Perera, S. B. (1981). *Descent to the goddess: A way of initiation for women.* Toronto: Inner City Books.

PART V

Nails, Tacks, and Hooks
Small but Essential

Nails, Tacks, and Hooks

The small items in this section are useful additions to any therapist's toolbox. You never know when you'll need a little nail to support the big picture, or a hook to hold a couple of ideas together. Sometimes, a tack will make just the right point. A few gadgets in the collection are mine; other fasteners and little bits of wisdom were gleaned from some of the best therapists, teachers, friends, and lovers I've been privileged to know. These offerings are little gifts to your clients from you. Sometimes, you ask a question that helps them address an issue; other times, you tell a story to illustrate a dynamic; and still other times, you share an anecdote to get a point across in a humorous way.

But What If You Did Know?

My friend Suzy Heer is one of the delights of my life. At one point in her varied life, she was a therapist, and the following is one of her techniques.

Many clients come to us because they just don't know what to do. They want answers, advice, and affection. Suzy would say, "OK, so you don't know what to do (or say), but what if you did? What if you did know what to do (or say)? What would you do (or say)?"

She used this little gem on me when I consulted her on an affair of the heart in my between-marriages days. I found myself conjuring up an answer, tricked as it were, by the technique. I answered my own question, which is just what we want for our clients.

The Cancer Ward

This is another Suzyism. It's most effective when dealing with a client who is wasting his or her life's blood and energy on a person or people who don't really matter in the long run. Sometimes it's hard to recognize such people. This technique shines a light on the relative importance of problematic family or friends.

Suzy says that when clients are agonizing, lamenting, and whining about their relationship with a person or people who are causing them grief, pose this question: If you had cancer and the long fight was almost over, and you were in the hospital dying, who would you want in the room with you?

If the person or people causing the grief are not on that list, something important has been learned.

What Would You Tell Your Girlfriend?

Paula Caplan, source for the Mother Interview (Chapter 26), is another one of my blessings. She is a psychologist, noted in her field as an educator, academician, public speaker, and author. The following is a great little item that she uses.

When your female client is agonizing over what to do about a difficult situation—her boyfriend is treating her poorly, a coworker humiliated her, she suspects her husband is cheating on her, or she saw her best friend's husband with another woman—and she looks at you pleadingly seeking advice, ask her this question: What would you say to a girlfriend who came to you with this story?

This question elicits responses that come from a deep place in a woman's psyche. It appeals to the sanctity of friendship between women and the long history of devotion that women friends have enjoyed. Girlfriends are loyal and honest and bonded powerfully to one another. Women know that boyfriends come and go, husbands come and go, children come and go, but girlfriends are forever. She will give her girlfriend (and thus, herself) the best advice ever.

The Forest Fire

It is common for a person seeking therapy to have saved up a lifetime of problems before that last one pushes him or her over the line and into your office. The comfortable side of the line is the familiar territory of "I can figure this out myself," and the other side of the line is not only asking for help but also paying for it. It is a quantum leap for many people.

By the time your poor client gets to your office, he or she is confused, overwhelmed, and frustrated by what may be a litany of difficulties. Where do you start? I suggest starting with a story, a metaphor about a forest fire.

> Imagine that you are at the foot of a mountain. Looking up, you see that a forest fire is blazing at the top of the tree line and is moving rapidly down the mountain. What do you do? It would be a Herculean task to address the raging wall of flames. You would need to call out all available firefighters. You would need helicopters to drop chemicals or water, and ground troops to march in from below. However, if you could somehow separate the fire into pieces, then separate it again and again into smaller and smaller pieces, you could walk over, pee on the little fires, and put them out all by yourself.

Having said that, the two of you can start on one of the issues that he or she brought to session.

The First Rule

Leon Bradshaw was one of my favorite professors in graduate school. He looks like Freud, but in character, he is more like Yoda. He has a ring of white hair and a neatly cropped beard the same color. His gentle and often mischievous eyes peer out from little round glasses. He is incredibly wise. He was a student of Carl Rogers, and he carries the torch passed on to him by the master with a certain light grace. He supports, challenges, and intrigues his students. They love him. He is also an excellent therapist.

One time, back in my grad school days, Dr. Bradshaw began his class with a question. "What is the first rule of therapy?" he asked us, folding his arms and leaning against the board in his characteristically casual way. Tentatively, a few hands went up.

"Is it to always have positive regard for the client?" posed the eager student.

"No" was the reply.

"That you should never impose your agenda on the client," another classmate offered.

"Nope."

"You should have a number of models for doing therapy to draw from and not depend on just one," another ventured.

"No."

"Could it be that your empathic skills, the ability to really 'be with' your client is the most important thing?" the frowning future therapist suggested.

"No."

Several more attempts were made, but each was dismissed with the now-predictable rejection. We were becoming uneasy and starting to shift around in our seats. We looked at one another, searching for a sign that one of us had the correct answer, but we only rolled our eyes and shrugged our shoulders to acknowledge defeat. Finally, we threw in the towel.

"The first rule of therapy," the wily professor stated as we all leaned forward in expectation, "is that the therapist must survive."

I have found that adage to be the most helpful thing I learned in grad school. It is absolutely true and particularly useful for those in the helping professions. Nurses, doctors, therapists, teachers, ministers, and others who devote their careers to service to others have a high rate of burnout. But they are not the only ones. Accountants, lawyers, mothers, fathers, sisters, construction workers, and cab drivers may also be at risk.

I use this little gem with my clients who are at risk of losing themselves in work, relationships, addiction, whatever. I ask them, "What is the first rule for (mothers, secretaries, soccer coaches, etc.)?" Make it hard, and make them guess. Let them struggle for a bit. Then, give the answer: "The (mother, secretary, soccer coach) must survive."

How Women Choose Men

I am tempted to make up an interesting story of how I learned this prize-winning parable, but the truth is, I can't remember where I got it. I use it all the time, in both individual therapy and couples work. If you time it just right, it can turn the tide in a couples session. There is probably something politically incorrect about it, but it's the unmitigated truth.

When a woman is choosing a man, it's as if she's looking over a herd of bulls. They are all standing together in the pasture, large, powerful, great horned specimens. She gazes intently over the herd, taking note. Then she spies one she likes. He stands out from the others; he's unique, different. She likes that and chooses him. Then, she spends the rest of her life trying to make him look like all the others. If she is successful, she doesn't want him anymore.

They Didn't Mean To

Honoring father and mother is a cultural norm. Many people are unwilling or unable to make an honest examination of the way they were parented because they are afraid to be critical of their mother or father. For some people, being critical of a parent feels so disloyal that it is almost impossible to allow into consciousness. Although parent bashing is seldom good therapy, neither is avoiding the reality that parents make mistakes, and mistakes have consequences. This story helps clients understand that negative parental behavior has consequences in a non-blaming way.

> What happened to you is like this: Imagine you are a little kid playing in the driveway of your home. The driveway slopes from the garage down to the street. The garage door is closed. Your mother needs to go to the grocery store, so she gets in the car and pushes the garage door opener. When the door is up, she looks in her rearview mirror, but she does not see you because of the driveway's slope. She even checks her side mirror, but again, because of the sloping driveway, she does not see you. Then, she puts the car in reverse and backs out. In the process, she runs over your legs. Your mother is horrified to see what she has done to you; hurting you is the last thing she intended. But your legs are no less broken because it was an accident.

Your Most Precious Natural Resource

Someone once told me that there were basically two kinds of people in life: plugs and receptacles. Receptacles were those people who are direct links to energy. They are the doers and achievers, the laughing and the loving, the giving and the gifted. Plugs are people who need a source of energy outside themselves. Plugs without receptacles are powerless. Plugs are constantly in search of receptacles, and when a receptacle is found, they attach themselves and drain the receptacle's energy. It's not a pretty picture, but the point is made.

Unfortunately, in the human condition, energy is not an unlimited resource. Each person has only so much. Sometimes, receptacles do not discriminate about who plugs into them. They allow random plugging in by whomever comes along, and their precious energy supply is depleted. Receptacles need to learn to cover their entries when not in use, and be discerning about who gets access.

This does not imply that receptacles make themselves unavailable to others, nor does it imply that they should be stingy or selfish. It simply means that they must learn to protect themselves from indiscriminate loss of energy.

Good Judgment

If you do much work with adolescents and their parents, you will certainly confront the overprotective parent. These days, one can understand the fears that accompany the launching of a child into adulthood; it's scary business. Events reported in the media every day convince parents that no one and no place is safe for their children anymore, not even their churches or schools. However, some well-meaning parents become their own worst enemies.

I was working with such a family one summer. Their 14-year-old daughter had them scared witless. Everything she did was suspect, from the music she liked to the friends she chose. Their fears were not groundless. The girl had pulled a few (mostly age-appropriate) indiscretions, such as sneaking out of the house when a girlfriend spent the night and paying a visit to the hot guy down the street who was a classmate. The girls were busted on the way back in, and grounded appropriately.

Then, her mother found a disturbing note in her daughter's backpack. A girlfriend was having sex and wrote all about it. The mother was horrified by the contents of the note.

Finally, the girl lied about attending church youth group one Sunday evening. She was at the church all right, but sneaked off with one of the older high school boys to do who-knows-what out behind the building.

With every episode, the parents pulled the reins tighter until the girl was pretty much locked up at home. The prisoner rioted. With teenagers, there's truth to the adage that the more you insist, the more they resist. The trick to parenting teens is to give them enough rope to grow, but not so much that they hang themselves. It's no easy feat! As I tried to help these parents see that their chosen course was leading right into a tornado, the mother kept saying, "But I cannot allow her to have freedoms and privileges until she learns good judgment!" or "She has to prove to us she has good judgment before she will be allowed to do this or that." Every time I tried to get the parents to loosen the grip a little, the "good judgment" theme surfaced. Then, one day, when I was on my way to the office, I switched on the radio just in time to hear a commentator say these words: "Good judgment comes from experience, and experience comes from bad judgment." I had no idea what the context for the statement was, but I didn't care. I pulled onto a side street as soon as possible, parked my car, and wrote down the wonderful words. They were so perfect for this family. The girl's parents had gone so far as to curtail their daughter's freedom that she had no room for experiences. The truth is, we have to allow for some bad experiences in life. If only we could teach experience!

Frankly, the wise words did not do much good with the family in question. They disappeared from therapy, probably because I would not tell them what they wanted to hear. But I have used the phrase with great success ever since and encourage you to drop it in your toolbox where you can find it easily.

The Dribble Theory of Happiness

I have to hand this one to Paula again. You might want to read another of her books, *The Myth of Women's Masochism* (referenced at the end of this section), for more information about the concept. Too bad I had to learn it from the University of Life rather than from reading her book or from attending classes at a nice, safe academic institution.

Many women have bought into a theory about happiness. We believe that if we can just fill that man's cup with happiness, all the way to the top, a little will dribble over the edge for us! Trouble is, it doesn't work.

Isn't that great? It is a jumping-off place from which you can begin to help your female clients see that they are the ones responsible for their happiness. A man's happiness is up to him as well. Of course, in a loving relationship, both partners should care about the other's happiness, but that is very different from taking responsibility for it. Note: Yes, this happens the other way around as well. Sometimes, it is a man who practices the Dribble Theory . . . but not as often!

Once a Pickle . . .

Bill Zaslow is a wonderful guy and a dear friend of my husband's and mine. He owns and operates a business that provides probation and parole services, as well as mediation service and substance abuse treatment.

He has been working with recovering (and not-so-recovering) substance abuse victims for years. I once worked in the field myself, and although I no longer work with substance abusers, I try to keep current with new discoveries in the field. Not long ago, I read an article promoting a study that indicated that controlled drinking was indeed possible for the alcoholic. I asked Bill about it. He smiled knowingly and said that controlled drinking was the fantasy of every alcoholic. He was dubious about the study and its findings. Then he said, "You know what happens when you put a cucumber in vinegar. After a while, it becomes a pickle.

Once a pickle, it can never be a cucumber again." I loved the metaphor and thought it was helpful. Bill said that it has been around in the recovering community for years, but I'd never heard it. I think it is a winner for your toolbox!

Sexual Tensions

I use this truism so often that I almost did not drop it in the toolbox, thinking that everyone must know about it. But in case everyone doesn't, I include it here.

This is an explanation for the age-old complaint by men that they don't get enough "physical contact" from their girlfriend or wife. Meanwhile, the girlfriend or wife is complaining that she and he are not "close."

The reality is that in order for women to feel like being sexual with their partners, we first want to feel emotionally close and intimate. But in order for men to feel like being emotionally close and intimate, they first want to be sexual. So, we come at the encounter from two completely different directions; frankly, it's amazing we ever get together at all!

Couples find this amazingly helpful. You don't give them an easy answer, but you normalize their dilemma.

Remember the behavioral "conditioning" processes that you studied in grad school? They work. I often see this result in practice: Women are conditioned to pull away when their partner approaches them with a gesture of touch. When touch—a hug, a pat, a gentle pinch, a kiss, a caress—usually leads to a sexual encounter, the gesture soon assumes a meaning all its own: If he touches me, I'm going to wind up flat on my back! So, of course, women start shrinking away when men make physical contact of any kind.

A task for the therapist is to do some teaching about emotional intimacy. One way to do that is to provide opportunities for emotional intimacy to occur in session (see Chapter 11, "The Couple's Love Story," and Chapter 17, "A Soulful Relationship"). Another way is to model emotional intimacy in your relationship with them. Then, you can work toward extinguishing the learned response of pulling away (see Chapter 14, "Resurrecting the Dead Relationship").

Real People

Charlotte Trautman was one of my supervisors for licensure, and we ended up being friends as well as colleagues. One time, I referred a couple to her. I had been seeing one partner in the duo, and working with both of them just seemed too great a task, so I sent them to Charlotte. My client returned after one of their couple sessions, amazed by Dr. Trautman's pronouncement. Cutting through the maze of complications and contradictions in the complicated couple, Charlotte, leaning forward in her chair, looked at them squarely and said, "Real people in real relationships have sex." Everything sort of fell into place after that.

I borrowed Charlotte's prophetic utterance and have used it many times. I think it deserves a spot in your toolbox.

Toothpaste

People often seek therapy when they are thinking about making a change in their lives, or in response to a change that appears like an uninvited guest. It seems that any kind of change is a challenge to the human spirit. One time, in the course of making one myself, I learned a valuable metaphor that I pass on to my clients whenever the opportunity allows. This bit of wisdom was a gift to me from one of my spiritual directors.

In the current spiritual revival, time-honored but long-forgotten customs, disciplines, and practices have been resurrected and are enjoying new life. People all over the country are walking labyrinths, signing up for yoga classes, learning tai chi, practicing meditation, joining spiritual friends groups, and listening to monks and nuns chant. Spiritual direction is an ancient tradition that, like others, has attracted renewed interest and attention in recent years.

Although the relationship of director and directee is not the same as the relationship between therapist and client, it is related. Spiritual directors are not licensed mental health professionals, although there are many programs and institutes that educate spiritual directors and offer certification. The director is a person whom the directee sees as a mentor, someone who is further down the spiritual path and might have more wisdom and insight. A spiritual director agrees to sit with his or her directee regularly, at an agreed-upon time and place, as a companion in the directee's spiritual journey. Some directors charge a fee for this service; some do not.

The Reverend Larry Lewis and his wife, Ruth, are my spiritual directors. We meet every month in the living room of their family home, a gracious Victorian that sits on a hill overlooking the small rural town of Osceola, Missouri. The wooden floors creak and give a bit as I make my way to one of the several rocking chairs positioned comfortably around the fireplace. The clock on the mantel ticks loudly as Larry prays us into the hour. Like therapy, sometimes, direction is sometimes a comfortable experience, sometimes not. I always learn something.

On one occasion, I was struggling with a transition in my life that involved making some tough decisions. I was in the same place that my clients often are when seeking my counsel. In this instance, I was feeling trapped, overwhelmed, and pulled in different directions by a variety of compelling forces. After I told my tale and lamented my predicament to my patient listeners, the three of us sat in silence. After a few minutes, Ruth, rocking slightly in her chair, offered this metaphor:

> I think you are like toothpaste in the tube. In order for any real movement to take place, the toothpaste must be squeezed from an external force. When being squeezed, the toothpaste gets crowded and cramped inside the tube. Finally, the pressure moves the toothpaste out of the tube. It is no different with you right now. You are feeling trapped and cramped, like there is not enough space in your life. You feel pressured and overwhelmed. Perhaps these feelings are necessary. Without them, you might not make the move that you need to make.

This idea enabled me to see that the move I was contemplating was, in all probability, a necessary one. The metaphor was so helpful that I began using it in therapy the very next day. I hope you will remember this handy little tool the next time you are working with a client in transition, and give it a try.

Suggested Reading

Guenther, M. (1992). *Holy listening: The art of spiritual direction*. Cambridge, MA: Cowley.

Resource

The Shalem Institute for Spiritual Formation: www.shalem.org.

About the Author

Susan E. Carrell, RN, LPC, is a therapist in private practice and owner of
Carrell Counseling, P.C., in Springfield,
Missouri. She is also the Episcopal chaplain for Southwest Missouri State University, Drury University, and Ozarks
Technical College. Previously, she was
a psychiatric nurse educator, as well as
a substance abuse counselor for adolescents in an inpatient treatment facility
and a psychiatric nurse clinician for hospitalized adolescents. She was also the
owner and director of a state-certified
alcohol and drug education program
for youth.

About the Artist

Jack Weins, MA, LPC, is a therapist in
private practice and owner of Allies for
Growth Counseling Services in Frisco,
Colorado. He is also a freelance artist
and does fine art painting and sculp-
turing.